MW01108296

A Touch of Torah

Divrei Torah, Midrashim, Poems and Essays

To Amy—
May this book
touch your heart!
Your friend,
Anne Lowe

Anne Lowe

Author and Illustrator

iUniverse®

A TOUCH OF TORAH
DIVREI TORAH, MIDRASHIM, POEMS AND ESSAYS

Pomegranate Folded Paper Art on cover and inside the book, by Anne Lowe

Photo of Pomegranate Art by Barry Sharoff

Stained Glass Art of "7 Days of Creation" used on the cover and and inside the book, courtesy of Congregation Bet Shalom, Tucson, AZ, B'nei Mitzvah class of 1998

Photograph of Anne Lowe courtesy of the Jewish Federation of Southern Arizona

The Sefarad Hebrew simulation font that is used in the Titles within this book and on the cover was designed by Juan-Jose Marcos, Professor of Classics, Plasencia, Spain

iUniverse books may be ordered through booksellers or by contacting:

iUniverse
1663 Liberty Drive
Bloomington, IN 47403
www.iuniverse.com
1-800-Authors (1-800-288-4677)

ISBN: 978-1-5320-5844-8 (sc)
ISBN: 978-1-5320-5846-2 (hc)
ISBN: 978-1-5320-5845-5 (e)

Library of Congress Control Number: 2018915122

Print information available on the last page.

iUniverse rev. date: 02/08/2019

Contents

Book of Leviticus

Book of Numbers

Book of Deuteronomy

A Bissel of This and a Bissel of That

Acknowledgments

Although it appears at the beginning of this book, I actually put off writing this section for fear of inadvertently leaving out any of my deserving friends, colleagues, and family members. I hope I do not offend anyone by an act of omission.

My first words of gratitude go to Lynn Saul, who taught me what it is to write a *midrash*; gave me a verbal, loving push about ten years ago to write and give my first D'var Torah; and was also my guide in two Jewish writing groups. You might say the rest is history! But I would be remiss if I didn't also credit her in encouraging me to come to Shabbat morning services at Congregation Bet Shalom in Tucson. At first I thought I would come maybe once a month. Then it progressed to twice a month. Now it is every Saturday that I am in Tucson and not traveling to visit grandchildren or attend a Hadassah conference. Thank you, Lynn.

Over five years ago, our synagogue made a big leap of faith from a lay-led congregation to one that hired a spiritual leader, Hazzan (Cantor) Avraham Alpert. Cantor Avi followed what Lynn started and asked me to present a D'var Torah every four to six weeks. I am grateful to him for his faith in my abilities and for his beautiful friendship. The fact that our congregation went on to ask him to become a rabbi, and his perseverance in doing so, is an example of his sterling character. Thank you, Rabbi Hazzan Avi.

A big *todah rabah* ("thank-you") also goes to the immediate past executive director of Congregation Bet Shalom, for her steadfast support and friendship. Thank you, Sarah Frieden!

I have lived in Tucson with my husband, David, for fourteen years, and I have made many close friends there. Virtually all of them make me feel special when they read/hear my writing or see my artwork. Thanks go out to the members of the Jewish Federation Northwest (a satellite facility of the Jewish Federation of Southern Arizona), currently led by Director Phyllis Gold, who, with Marti Cohen, Sarah Chen (who has recently moved to Louisiana), and Carol Nudelman, have invited me to share my writings with the Rosh Chodesh ladies there. I also thank the Northwest Federation/Hadassah Southern Arizona Book Club, recently chaired by Sandra Reino, for giving me magnificent support. Thank you, ladies.

My dear friends at Congregation Bet Shalom always keep me buoyed up and floating on air when I deliver a D'var Torah, and they greet me at my seat when I return from the *bima*, with handshakes and words of praise. I must mention a few who have been my supporters from day one. Thank you, Reverend Dr. Norman Rubin and Kathy McGuire Rubin, who rush in from the kitchen, where there are preparing Kiddush, whenever I start to give a D'var Torah. The same thanks go out to Nadya and Moshe Garfein, Vivien and Jacques Gerstenfeld, Stephanie and David Mack, Andy and Linda Kunsberg, Louise Good, Amy Rangel Stymiest, Elinor and Bernie Engelhard, Talya Fanger-Vexler, Kamala Alpert, Teri and Ole Thienhaus, Sid Temlock, and so many more. Thank you, friends and fellow congregants.

Close friends in the Tucson area who have always encouraged me in my writing are Ruth Beecher, Ruth and Jim Barwick, and Barbara Esmond (especially late at night!). It seems that I can tell you anything and you always give me good advice. The same goes for Mary Ellen Loebl, the PJ

Library coordinator for the Jewish Federation of Southern Arizona. Thank you, friends.

It seems that the more I list those who tell me my writing is special, the more people I think of to thank. I am blessed with wonderful friends who continually encourage me, such as Phyllis Braun, editor of the *Arizona Jewish Post,* and Shira Brandenburg, the immediate past director of the Tucson International Jewish Film Festival. Thank you, Phyllis and Shira.

And so I now come to my family—always supportive, always loving, always proud of my efforts. To my three children and their spouses: Jonathan and Monique Lowe, Caren and Doug Elenowitz, and Ethan and Mitten Lowe, merci beaucoup for being you and for loving me. To my grandchildren— Shailah, Jordan, Alexandra, and Jacob Lowe; Evan and Abigail Elenowitz; and Helena and Emmet Lowe—I love you, and I thank you for making Grannie Annie always welcome in your hearts. And to my husband, David E. Lowe, who is ever supportive and ever accepting of my constant "projects," including the compiling of this book, thank you for being here by my side for nearly fifty years and for loving me in all my endeavors. Thank you to all my family.

Preface

For about ten years, I have been writing and giving a D'var Torah every month or so for my conservative Jewish congregation, Bet Shalom, in Tucson, Arizona. *D'var* means "word" or "talk." A D'var Torah is a talk that has its basis in the Torah. A weekly D'var Torah usually is derived from the portion (*parasha*) of the Torah that is read on Saturday.

Over the years, I have accumulated a goodly amount of these talks, and so many of my fellow congregants have pushed me to actually publish these that I decided to do so! I do not have a D'var Torah for every parasha, and in some cases I actually have two or more that I have written on a single portion. Some of these start out the same way for a paragraph or two, and then they go in a different direction from each other. Sometimes a D'var Torah is based on a verse, a thought, or even a title of the parasha. When I read the portion, I find something that tickles my intellect, and off I go.

My main objective is to make Torah alive today, to find something that resonates in our modern world. Some of you may agree with my conjectures, and some of you may not. My goal is to clarify to myself what the Torah teaches me and then to convey that to others. I have found that many of my non-Jewish friends also find these writings to have meaning for them as people of many diverse faiths.

In addition to these Divrei Torah (*Divrei* is the plural of D'var), I have added poems, *midrashim* (plural of *midrash* and meaning "legends" or "stories"), and essays that have a connection to the parasha. Since I have been a member of a Jewish writing group for a long time, I also have some vignettes and other writings that will come at the end of this book, in the section "A Bissel of This and a Bissel of That," which is a little bit of a nod to my Yiddish-speaking parents and grandparents.

I make no claim to being a Jewish spiritual leader. I am not a rabbi or a cantor—nor am I a Jewish educational professional. I am merely a Jewish woman who is trying to understand her place in the Jewish world and also trying to grasp the intricacies of Torah. At one time, I thought of writing an ethical will for my children and grandchildren. Instead, I think they will understand how I feel about being a good person just by reading these writings of mine. I hope they—and you—will find merit in *A Touch of Torah*.

—Anne Lowe

Book of Genesis

D'var Torah for Bereshis

When I said that I would give a D'var Torah for today, October 22, 2011, I actually didn't realize that it would be for the parasha Bereshis. What an honor to do this today, when we start to read the Torah all over again from the very beginning!

Today we hear that powerful story of Creation, the story that every Jewish or Christian child hears repeatedly throughout his or her religious education. Indeed, the story that we read right after Simchat Torah each year, such as we are going to do today. Other cultures, such as our Native American tribes, have equally compelling stories about the origins of the earth and of humankind, but we cling to ours, even when Darwin's theory of evolution chides us that seven days should really be ages. So what's a few eras, or eons, between friends? It's still a riveting story with graphic images and infinite possibilities for midrashim.

In fact, every time I sit in my seat in this *shul*, I always gaze with an artist's eyes at the images in stained glass right here over our ark. Have you noticed, as I have, the lovely blue ribbon of glass that flows from one panel to the next? It's kind of a tie that holds these seven days together. It starts with day one, with the wind—the *ruach*, or spirit of G-d—sweeping over

1

the water. "Let there be light." Do you see the royal blue? In Italian, that blue is called *azurro*. I love saying that word.

The ribbon of blue—or azurro—continues into the second day, the third, the fourth, the fifth, and the sixth, and all the way across, even into the Sabbath, the seventh day. So when I am here, I think of the story of Creation as having a blue tinge. Indeed, if you are lucky enough to be an astronaut, when you look down from space at our earth, it appears as a big blue marble.

When a baby is born, the umbilical cord sometimes appears to have a blue color to it, on account of the three blood vessels within it: two arteries and one vein. And why do newborn babies always have blue eyes for a while?

Blue is also one of the three colors used for the linen and wool drapings made for the Mishkan, the Tabernacle to hold the Ark of the Covenant. The other two colors are red and purple, very close to blue in the colors of a prism.

And then we have the direction in our prayer books to tie a blue thread in the corner of our *tsitsis,* or prayer shawls. If you look at your *talesim,* you do not see this. Apparently, there was a special mollusk used to produce this color in biblical times. Since it is uncertain whether this exact mollusk is still in existence, we do not have that blue thread ... yet! Who knows what may be found as archaeology continues to make discoveries?

What about the flag of Israel? Again, we have two ribbons of blue, on top and bottom. Blue, the color of the creation of the state of Israel.

When my husband and I were married, forty-two years ago, a popular song at the time was "L'amour est bleu," or "Love Is Blue." What could better illustrate the story of Creation than a couple dancing to the song "Love Is Blue" on their wedding day? As we read in this parasha, in 2:18, the Lord G-d said, "It is not good for man to be alone. I will make a fitting helper for him."

Two weeks ago, at the Northwest Division of the Jewish Federation of Southern Arizona and Hadassah Southern Arizona Book Club meeting, we discussed the book *The Sparrow* by Mary Doria Russell. This author is a woman who had a Jesuit upbringing and schooling but later in life converted to Judaism. She has penned a compelling story of a small group of people who travel to another planet. The majority of the members of this mission were Jesuit priests (perhaps modern-day Father Kinos?). One of the space travelers is a Sephardic Jewish woman.

One of the members of our book club asked how the Jesuits could reconcile their find on this planet, called Rakhat, with their belief in the story of Creation, our Bereshis. They found two races of sentient beings on Rakhat: a master race and a submissive and gentle race, which was dominated in a horrible way by the masters.

I suggested that we look at Bereshis for an answer to this question. Every time G-d made another day, he "saw that it was good." In fact, in 1:31, "And God saw all that He had made, and found it VERY good."

Perhaps G-d had made Rakhat *before* he made our planet but found it not so good, with one horrible race subjugating another one. Maybe that might be why he started again with our Garden of Eden, with Adam and Eve.

So I ask you, Are we any better in our world today? Are we all doing our part to make the world good again as it was in Eden? A very daunting task.

At the risk of you thinking I am totally into stickers, since I gave you the Keep Tucson Kind stickers when I gave a D'var Torah a few weeks ago, I am going to give you another sticker. This one is to remind us to try to return to the goodness that G-d created when he made humans in the story of Creation.

This sticker is from the Fund for Civility, Respect, and Understanding and was created by the family of Ron Barber, who was shot during the Gabrielle Giffords tragedy last January. I have a paper about this project that you can pick up too, if you are interested.

By the way, the sticker is blue.

Shabbat Shalom!

Another D'var Torah for Bereshis

I was checking in my computer files, and I saw that I also did a D'var Torah last year for Bereshis. In that one, I bade you all to look at the windows behind me, at the images in stained glass right here behind our ark, at the lovely blue ribbon of glass that flows from one glass panel to the next. I described it as a tie that holds these seven days together. It starts with day one, with the wind—the ruach, or spirit of G-d—sweeping over the water. "Let there be light." Do you see the royal blue? The ribbon continues from one day to the next, all the way across, even into the Sabbath, the seventh day.

My D'var from last year continued to talk about the color blue, but today I will take a different path. In fact, with your indulgence, I hope to be somewhat sacrilegious!

We read today about the Garden of Eden, which many refer to as a paradise. In this garden, Adam and his helpmate, Eve, started their existence. In this Gan Eden, "the Lord God caused to sprout from the ground every tree pleasant to see and good to eat, and the Tree of Life in the midst of the garden, and the Tree of Knowledge of good and evil."

So I'd like you to think for a moment: Would you be content in the Garden of Eden if you were Adam or Eve? There were abundant fruit and vegetables, all provided by the Lord. You did no labor to produce your food. You were naked because you had no modesty, and it must have been a perfect temperature year-round because, otherwise, you would need some protective clothing. You only had one human being with whom to converse. There were no books, magazines, video games, DVDs, Facebook friends, cinemas, universities, plays, operas, or athletic events. Watching the Olympics was eons in the future.

I propose to you that, just maybe, Adam and Eve might have been a trifle bored. Paradise, of course, is different for everyone. I once took a stress-management course (it didn't help) where we were asked to imagine ourselves in a perfect place, doing the most enjoyable thing we could imagine. Nearly everyone in the class spoke of lying on a white sandy beach by an exquisite deep-blue ocean (maybe Tahiti?), drinking a Polynesian concoction, and totally vegging out.

When it was my turn to tell of my perfect day, I sheepishly said that I'd like to be in bed, with a soaking rain coming down outside, reading a great book at least nine hundred pages long. I know there were plenty of people in the class rolling their eyes at my nerdy vision of paradise.

Yet I wonder if, to Eve and Adam, their Garden of Eden lacked that which makes life worthwhile. Where was the challenge in their days? Where was the feeling of accomplishment of a task well done? What did they do when they had the creative urge to be artistic? Did Eve make a crown of dandelions for Adam? Sadly, it would not last long.

So I think that when the serpent urged her to defy G-d and taste of the Tree of Knowledge, she may have been secretly glad. Just a few words of enticement from the serpent did her in, and then, of course, she needed a partner in crime, and Adam did not fail her. Maybe the crime was not totally theirs alone. Perhaps part of their misbehavior and disregard for G-d's rule of not eating from that tree can be attributed to the fact that paradise isn't all that it's cracked up to be.

So I ask you to think about what your perfect Gan Eden, or paradise, would be. Would you opt for no work, all play, no intellectual pursuits, and no friends other than your mate and the animals around you? Or would you want a different garden?

You probably noticed that I brought up a bag with me. I did not bring Scotch whiskey this time, but I hope I have enough apples here for everyone. We'll put them out at the Kiddush. When you bite into your apple, think about the Garden of Eden and what you might call paradise.

Shabbat Shalom!

Eve's Bite

As she took that first tentative bite of the beckoning fruit, Eve tasted
regret;
remorse;
guilt; and,
surprisingly, a touch of exhilaration.

Every synapse in her body was aroused and set off sparks of
awareness;
excitement;
desire; and,
surprisingly, modesty.

Her tongue was enlivened with pinpoints of fiery sensations of
pain;
spice;
sensitivity; and,
surprisingly, a feeling of change.

She touched the tip of her tongue with her little finger, finding it
moist;
hot;
alive; and,
surprisingly, slightly indented, with two ends.

Eve ran to Adam, with juice dripping down her chin, beckoning him to
partake;
misbehave; and
awaken, and,
surprisingly, her speech had a sibilant quality.

Adam succumbed to her wishes, and ate of the forbidden morsel, to find knowledge;
sensitivity;
shame; and,
surprisingly, that his skin had developed a faint diamond pattern that throbbed.

The two were expelled from the Garden, taking with them
hunger;
commitment;
loss; and,
surprisingly, a deep love for each other, fueled by new insights.

Simchat Torah
Jellied-Apple Memories

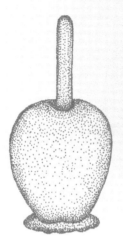

In the Kiddush room of the shul, they awaited the fray:
Popsicle-stick sentinels on a stainless steel tray.
Translucent red coats of tooth-chipping ability,
Who cared at all for enamel's fragility?
Macintosh tartness covered with a thick hard glaze,
Nearly impossible to eat: That did not faze.
"Daddy, will you start mine, please?"
He'd pick up my apple and crunch in with ease.
Walking home, we'd munch in a delighted sugar high,
With cheeks and chins covered in scarlet sticky dye.
The reading of the Torah began before we chewed.
Sweet taste of our heritage: rosy-red hued!

D'var Torah for Noah

Today we read the parasha of Noah, a story that is told to every Jewish child, and to children of some other faiths as well. It is a popular story, and even entire baby nurseries are decorated with the theme. Yet this tale is grim, full of the Lord's disappointment with the people on the earth, to the extent that he destroys everyone but Noah and his immediate family. It makes a person wonder why it would be a good story for children. Indeed, it seems hardly appropriate for a baby's bedroom! Nevertheless, the covenant that Ha-Shem makes at the end of the flood, sealed by the arrival of a rainbow, is one of forgiveness for all eternity.

In Genesis 9:12- 9:15, G-d states,

> This is the sign that I set for the covenant between Me and you, and every living creature with you, for all ages to come. I have set My bow in the clouds, and it shall serve as a sign of the covenant between Me and the earth. When I bring clouds over the earth, and the bow appears in the clouds, I will remember My covenant between Me and you and every living creature among all flesh, so that the waters shall never become a flood to destroy all flesh.

How many of you have caught your breath in pleasure when you see a rainbow in the sky? Don't you immediately nudge the person next to you and say, "Look! There's a rainbow?" It is a fairly rare phenomenon that delights the beholder. But do we remember what it means between G-d and the people of the earth?

In addition, in this parasha, we have the lovely vision of a white dove returning to the ark, its beak bearing an olive branch, a universal symbol of peace.

And just as a rainbow is seen by all humankind, Jewish or not, as a covenant, there are others in this world who are filled with reverence from the story of Noah. How many of you here have heard of the Noahide, Noahite, or Noachide Laws (also referred to as the Seven Laws of Noah)? Or the Noahide Nation?

A few years ago, as the director of outreach for the Jewish Federation and the JCC, I received a phone call from a gentleman who was moving to Tucson. He said he practiced the Noahide Laws, but was looking to convert to Judaism, as a result of studying more about these laws and the origins of Judaism. At the time, I had never heard of these laws, but I quickly studied up on them.

They are a set of moral imperatives that, according to the Talmud, were given by G-d as a binding set of laws for the "children of Noah," whom we understand to be all of humanity. Therefore, any non-Jew who adheres to these laws is regarded as a righteous gentile and is assured of a place in the world to come (Olam Haba), the final reward of the righteous.

According to Wikipedia and to many other internet sources, the seven laws are listed by the Tosefta (dated to 220 CE) and the Babylonian Talmud (dated to 300 CE):

1. The prohibition of idolatry
2. The prohibition of murder
3. The prohibition of theft
4. The prohibition of sexual immorality

5. The prohibition of blasphemy
6. The prohibition of eating flesh taken from an animal while it is still alive
7. The requirement of maintaining courts to provide legal recourse

These sound very similar to some of the Ten Commandments. Although the sixth one—the prohibition of eating flesh taken from an animal while it is still alive—is something rather different from what we Jews abide by, we are also prohibited from eating the blood of an animal. This comes from this same parasha, Genesis 9:4, where it is written, "You must not however, eat flesh with its life-blood in it." This is from where the sixth of the Noahide Laws derives.

But I can't even imagine eating something that might still be wiggling! I tried to think of an instance where this would occur, and all I could think of was the strange 1920s and '30s fad of swallowing a goldfish whole, while it was still alive. Yuck!

Also, one finds in Wikipedia, that in 1987, President Ronald Reagan signed a proclamation speaking of "the historical tradition of ethical values and principles, which have been the bedrock of society from the dawn of civilization when they were known as the Seven Noahide Laws, transmitted through God to Moses on Mount Sinai," and in 1991, the US Congress did the same.

I find it interesting that, at Yad Vashem, (yadvashem.org) the Holocaust Memorial in Israel, there are trees planted in the memory of the "Righteous Among the Nations." These were the non-Jewish people who had the courage to help Jews in Europe during the Nazi Holocaust, at risk of their own lives and livelihoods. Contrary to the general population of that time, these rescuers saw Jews as fellow human beings. Although the term Noahide would not have been used then, they were very obviously Noahides.

So are Jews considered Noahides? After all, they are also descendants of Noah. Actually, no, because this is a category for Gentiles only. The Noahide Laws were revealed long before Abraham. We Jews are descendants of Abraham through Isaac and Jacob, with our own covenant and mission to the world. As expressed in the Torah and revealed to Moses at Mount Sinai, Israel is to be separate from "the nations" (Numbers 23:9; Exodus 19:5–6).

But it doesn't mean we can go out and swallow a live goldfish!

So you must have seen me carry this bag up to the bima. And many of you know that I am fond of using props when I do a D'var Torah. Well, have no fear, I am not going to bring out a goldfish or two, or ask anyone to swallow it! Instead, I have some jars of olives for you to enjoy at the Kiddush today. So when you enjoy an olive or two, remember the white dove of peace that brought the olive branch back to Noah. Have a peaceful Shabbat and week to come.

Shabbat Shalom!

Porcupine on Noah's Ark

When on a perpetually overcrowded ark, where do I, a lap-sized denizen, park?

I can just stroll at a snail's pace, and legs will part to give me space.

Elephants will sidle to one side. Tigers will snarl and quietly hide.

Giraffes will be careful where they stepped. Frogs look twice before they leapt.

Serpents s-s-s-slither far away. Mama lions keep their cubs at bay.

Even the skunks clear a path for me. I am feared more than they, you see!

I blithely sashay over ribs of gopher wood. Just because I could!

Only my mate greets me with a smile so fine. No one else cares to embrace a porcupine.

D'var Torah for Lech Lecha

When Lynn Saul asked me to prepare a D'var Torah for this week's parasha, she said that Lech Lecha is sometimes considered the most interesting or fascinating parasha in the whole Torah. *Wow!* That's both exciting and daunting. Not being a rabbinic scholar, only a mere mortal who has just starting getting interested in Torah in the last three years, I hope that I will not let you down.

Lech Lecha has been translated into many different interpretations, including "go forth" or "betake yourself." It is a fairly lengthy parasha, which starts with Abram (before he becomes Abraham) and Sarai (before she becomes Sarah) heeding G-d's words to "go forth from your native land and from your father's house to the land that I will show you."

As soon as I read this phrase, I thought of this state of Arizona in which we live, which, coincidentally, is a desert, like the land of Canaan to which G-d sends Abram and Sarai. Would any of you who are native Tucsonans please stand up? So the rest of us have left our native states or countries to migrate here. Please sit down. Thank you.

A good many of us came here for various reasons. My husband and I came to be with our youngest son and his wife because they were going to have a child and they convinced us that they wanted grandparents nearby. So we packed up and moved here six years ago from Wisconsin. Then, two and a half years later, they moved to Boulder, Colorado. But we stayed in Tucson. We'd had enough of Lech Lecha, betaking ourselves!

I heard Nathan Frankenberg's mother speak here, telling the Hadassah chapter all about growing up Jewish in Paraguay. If I remember correctly, she said that the men of each family, escaping to Paraguay from Hitler, were each given a machete when they arrived in that South American nation from Europe, and told to hack out their home from the Paraguayan jungle.

I imagine it must have seemed just as foreign to Abram—not to mention, an incredibly awesome task—to go to Canaan from Ur, which is actually Iraq. It is pointed out in our Etz Hayim Chumashim (*Etz Hayim Torah and Commentary,* p.70) that this was the first time that a journey was undertaken, not as an exile, such as from the Garden of Eden, or the sending away of Cain, but as a response to a divine imperative. Abram was doing the bidding of the Lord.

Most immigrants leave their native lands because of religious persecution or to seek a better economic situation or, perhaps, to escape a repressive government. Indeed, the Mexican people who come to Arizona or other US states seek to better themselves and their families with sustainable work. This is not the case with Abram. He followed the Lord's dictates, and Sarai complied with his demands to go to a new land to follow the one G-d. They certainly weren't going to Canaan to be with children or grandchildren, because they hadn't had any yet … and Abram was already seventy-five years old! So we must give them their due—they were real pioneers, adventurers, and believers in the divine presence. I ask you all, "Would you leave the US to go to another country just because you heard a voice telling you to do so? Or would you call the nearest psychiatrist to make an appointment?"

Shabbat Shalom!

Hagar

I love words. I love to make words from words. If you take the name Hagar and make other English words from its letters, there is a never-ending source of thoughts and suggestions that arises.

For instance, the first three letters spell *hag*. Not a very pretty word. It connotes an ugly old crone. Maybe the witch in Hansel and Gretel. Does Hagar deserve this image? I think not. Let's abandon this word and move on.

If the letter *h* in *hag* is exchanged for another of the letters in Hagar's name, the *r*, then the word *rag* is formed. *Rag* leads the mind to *schmattah*, its Yiddish equivalent. Then the mind jumps to the old definition of *schmattah*: "A dress your husband's ex-wife is wearing." Well, Hagar *was* Abraham's ex-wife, in regard to Sarah. Again, a very churlish image.

Regard the last four letters of her name, *a-g-a-r*. A serious crossword puzzle devotee will undoubtedly know that *agar* is the word for a gelatin-like product of certain seaweeds, used for solidifying culture media. It is what is used in petri dishes to grow bacteria, molds, and so on. Remember that even though the word *bacteria* conjures up images of anthrax, meningitis, and other harmful diseases, there are good bacteria too. That is why yogurt is so indicated for the intestinal system: it restores bacteria that are beneficial to the digestive system.

And just think of molds! Not all molds are harmful, colorful formations from too-long-refrigerated food items. Some molds, like penicillin, cure diseases. So agar is a laboratory friend. It promotes the growth of tiny microorganisms, spores, and so forth.

Rah can also be formed from three of the letters in Hagar. Now we are moving into more pleasant territory. This is a cheer. No doubt, when we read in the Torah that the Lord saved Hagar and Ishmael in the desert, our minds gave a little cheer. It is difficult to think that Isaac became a patriarch, while his half brother Ishmael died from being cast out. Hur*rah* for letting him live.

So parts of Hagar's name conjure up words of dubious character, while other parts have a positive connotation. Is this because we do not know how to categorize Hagar herself? Was she not the loving mother of Ishmael and dutiful wife to Abraham? Or was she the mother who left her son to possibly die alone in the desert? No doubt she is a dichotomy—like everyone else in the world.

Now what would an Israeli do with Hagar's name in Hebrew?

D'var Torah for Vayera

This parasha, Vayera (meaning "He appeared"), refers to the Lord appearing to Abraham as he is recovering from his circumcision. In this parasha, we are told of the many trials that our patriarch experienced, to show how worthy he was to foster the Jewish people. Some of these trials—such as the final one, the possible sacrifice of his son Isaac—are incredibly difficult to understand. Perhaps Abraham's faith was so much greater than any of our, that we have our own trials in trying to grasp his magnificent faith in the Lord.

This parasha also tells of the wonderful story of Sarah laughing to hear she will become a mother at age ninety. No doubt, any of us would have laughed in bewilderment at this prophecy if we heard it about ourselves or another woman of this age.

There is a provocative novel out, entitled *State of Wonder,* by Ann Patchett. This book explores the possibility of women conceiving into their seventies, and even eighties, by chewing the bark of a tree in the Amazon rain forest. Far-fetched? Maybe. Maybe not. Read the book, and decide for yourself!

I wrote a few poems when I was part of Lynn Saul's Bet Shalom writing group, back in 2008 through 2012. I would like to share them with you today. The first two have to do with the announcement I was just talking about: Sarah and Abraham becoming parents very late in life.

Also in this parasha, toward the end, we learn of Sarah's jealousy of Hagar, of Hagar's son Ishmael, and of Sarah forcing Abraham to send them into the desert, where they nearly perished. It doesn't make me too pleased that Sarah is a matriarch of our religion and that she is so revered. On the other hand, it reveals to us that she is just as we are. She has normal traits and faults; she is not superhuman, even though Abraham appears to be. Perhaps we should look at her as someone to remind us of our own failings. Even as we commit indiscretions, we are human, just like she is, and can be forgiven.

My third poem is about Hagar, and how her being cast out may have implications even today. Some of you may remember these poems from ones that were handed out in the chapbooks that Lynn produced for the High Holidays a few years ago. If so, I hope you will understand that, even as our Torah is eternal, and we reread it year after year, we may also take pleasure in hearing or reading a poem more than once. I hope you enjoy listening to them, even for a second or third time, as much as I enjoyed writing them.

Shabbat Shalom!

Yitzchak (Laughter)

Genesis 18:12

When Abraham was eighty-seven, Hagar the maid, delivered his son;
But Sarah, at ninety, had given him none.

So laughter became the Viagra of yore,
Producing the spark of life Sarah bore.

Abraham laughed that his wife could conceive;
Sarah laughed that pleasure she'd receive.

Two very gray panthers lay together once more,
And through mirth did they form a core

Of a people both great and numerous beyond thought.
Gee, what a giggle or a chuckle had brought!

Sarah Laughed

Because Sarah laughed,
Her womb relaxed.
Receiving the seed,
It held on fast.

From a chuckle it grew
where there had been no issue.
And there were years
of misery to undo.

Could a giggle begin to heal,
When jealousy was all she could feel?
Would a child within her belly
turn dolor to zeal?

And would Abraham laugh at her,
At changes her old body would incur?
Or would his eyes portray joy
when his son's birth did occur?

Hagar and the Bee

Genesis 21:10
"Cast out that slave-woman and her son"

Hagar and son Ishmael, Abraham cast out.
She, in shock, sucked in a great gasp of air.
A honeybee was flying close about;
It was swallowed, unaware.

Worming its way from lungs to heart,
That bee crawled into the pumping cage.
It stung and left its toxic dart,
So Hagar's soul was filled with rage.

In Gaza and Nablus are Hagar's seed,
Retaining that poison from her breast.
"Death to Israel" has become their creed,
Bringing hatred to a fiery crest.

How terribly sad! That heart was stung!
Why couldn't that bee have brought instead
A deposit of nectar that would have clung
To bones and blood, torso and head?

Now honeybees are disappearing from earth,
And Hagar's minions have venom within.
Is this because one bee gave birth
To a cause it seems no one can win?

23

Vayera Midrash

The household was finally resuming a normal, peaceful demeanor. The upheaval of all the circumcisions was fading away. The men and boys were healing. The preparation of the soothing salves was finished, and there were no fevers or illnesses from the deeds. It was time to catch their breath.

Yet Abraham appears and demands that I make cakes of choice flour. Will this man ever give me a moment of rest? I am not a young bride with energy unlimited. I have seen ninety years, and my body is withered. But I can still make delicious cakes for unknown visitors!

I wipe my brow with the back of my mottled hand. But what is this? A brittle gray hair falls into the bowl of dough. I carefully pick it out and stare at it as it lays on my palm. In amazement, I watch it wind into a curl like that of a baby. It becomes not one shaft of hair, but duplicates itself again and again, and turns to light brown. Soon it is as soft and as full as the curl a mother would save from her child's first haircut. I tentatively stroke it and set it aside as I prepare the cakes, and then I bring them, golden and glowing, to the strangers.

Every few minutes, I go over to where I have placed the curl by the flour bags. It is still baby-fine, bountiful of follicles. It cannot be from my old pate. Yet there is no one else here in the tent with me.

Abraham is talking with the three visitors. Can I believe what I am hearing? He and I will have a child by next year! What a joke! As I chuckle, I look at the curl of hair. Right before my eyes, the strands begin to twist together into a perfect ring of braided hair, I am almost afraid to do so, but I pick it up with my right thumb and index finger. There is no end or beginning to the ring. It is fused together like fine metal. I slip it onto the fourth finger of my left hand, and now I truly laugh.

D'var Torah for Chayyei Sarah

Lynn Saul has taught me that it is necessary to read a parasha a few times before writing a D'var Torah about it, in order to find some key phrase, idea, or even a single word that resonates within the psyche. That is the jumping off point needed to write a personal commentary about a parasha.

So I read Chayyei Sarah a number of times. Indeed, it was last year that I had this very same parasha to wrangle with for my first D'var Torah about it. If some of you remember, I urged you to consider buying a burial plot for yourselves, as Abraham does for Sarah and himself in this section of the Torah.

Well, once again, I have been drawn to the purchase of burial plots by Abraham in this parasha. Abraham has chosen the Cave of Machpelah as the place he would like to spend eternity with Sarah. It belongs to Ephron, a Hittite, and it is near Mamre, which is now Hebron. Abraham is told twice by Ephron (or his emissaries) that the land he desires will be a gift to him, and he need not purchase it.

But Abraham insists on paying the four hundred shekels of silver for the land. He says, in 23:13, "If only you would hear me out! Let me pay the price of the land; accept it from me, that I may bury my dead there." Ephron agrees to let Abraham buy the cave and the field around it, rather than accept it as a gift.

How wise Abraham was to make this a binding agreement, comparable to a deed for the land! Even in his sorrowful state of mourning for Sarah, he knew that he was setting a solid business example for generations to come. Indeed, in the late 1800s and early 1900s, as the Jewish settlers from Europe started buying land in Palestine as *chalutzim* (pioneers who settled the future state of Israel), they showed that they had learned this lesson well from Abraham. They definitely bought the lands they settled from Arab landowners. Everything was above board, legal, and deeded. There are cases now where the Arabs are ruing these sales of decades past.

Did you know that some of the coins you and your parents and grandparents so diligently dropped into the blue *pushkes,* or JNF boxes, were used by the Jewish National Fund, also called Keren Kayemet, to purchase these lands? At those times, they were often malaria-infested swamplands, but those savvy chalutzim knew how to drain swamps and then turn them into healthy fields for crops, homesites, or even cities.

So we must thank Abraham. Not just for his acceptance of the one G-d, which led him to being our patriarch, but also for setting an example as a shrewd businessman so that someday the land of Israel would be ours.

I also inwardly chuckled that it definitely states in this parasha that the price for the cave and field was "four hundred shekels *at the going merchants' rate*" (23:16 [italics mine]). No one here was gouged; no one here was shorted. Everyone received a square deal for the sale and the purchase of the land. No real-estate agents received 6 percent of the sale. Everything was businesslike between two gentlemen, and totally fair. Again, another example to Abraham's descendants on how to conduct property sales that should stand the test of centuries to come. I am now wondering who lays claim to the Cave of Machpelah right now?! I imagine it would not be too difficult to find out.

I had originally mentioned to Lynn that I was going to write about the title of this parasha, Chayyei Sarah, or Life of Sarah. I guess I'll have to be assigned this parasha at least one more time in order to get to that ... maybe next year!

Shabbat Shalom!

Another D'var Torah for Chayyei Sarah:

"Won't You Be My Neighbor?"

When I agreed to give the D'var Torah this morning, I did not realize that I had done so for this parasha two times already in the past few years. In fact, while reading the one I had given in 2008, I decided to repeat many of the thoughts that I had expressed previously but to embellish this talk with some other ideas.

This Torah parasha, Chayyei Sarah, means the "Life of Sarah." Nevertheless, it begins with the death of our first matriarch, Sarah, the wife of Abraham. Sarah died in Hebron, and the simple phrases that convey Abraham's grief—such as "Abraham proceeded to mourn for Sarah" and "to bewail her," and "Abraham rose from beside his dead"—are more than enough to bring tears to the eyes and a catch to the throat, as we empathize with Abraham, a man like any other, who is racked by sorrow over the loss of his lifelong partner.

Then, in his dolor, he must choose a burial place and hope that he can convince the Ephron the Hittite to sell him the parcel, the Cave of

Machpelah. Indeed, through gentle negotiations, this purchase occurs. You might say that this is one of the first instances of creating sanctified ground for a Jewish burial. (As an aside, did you know that even limbs or pieces of the body, can also buried in sanctified ground?)

In Israel, there is the organization called ZAKA, which is perhaps best known for its sacred yet grisly work of collecting human remains to ensure a proper Jewish burial. ZAKA is active in the fields of emergency response (using motorcycles equipped with first-aid and firefighting equipment), search and rescue (including specialized canine units, divers, and rappelling units), and accident prevention.

Recognized by the United Nations in 2005 as an international humanitarian organization, ZAKA will send highly trained volunteers to assist in international disasters, working in conjunction with other emergency personnel. ZAKA volunteers have been seen among the first responders at the tsunami in Japan, the plane crash in Phuket, Hurricane Katrina, the *Columbia* space-shuttle disaster, the earthquake in Haiti, and terror attacks in Turkey, Mombasa, and Taba, among other catastrophes.

ZAKA is the Hebrew acronym for Disaster Victim Identification. Although victim identification is the organization's namesake, it is only one of the many services that ZAKA volunteers undertake following an incident.

On the internet I came across a statement from Motti, a member of the Chevra Kaddisha of ZAKA (the Chevra Kaddisha is the Jewish Burial Society): "We collect every drop of blood and the smallest piece of a body. Every time a blood vessel bursts there is a cascade of blood. We have special materials that help absorb this blood for burial."

So when the ZAKA volunteers find parts of bodies after terrorist bombings, they are buried in Jewish sanctified grounds.

I grew up in Saratoga Springs, New York, a small community of about fourteen thousand residents, north of Albany. During my childhood, two hundred Jewish families made up the congregation of the only synagogue in the city. It was named Shaarei Tefillah; in English, Gates of Prayer. It was an orthodox shul.

My parents were very active in the synagogue, and, for as long as I can remember, my dad was the chair of the Cemetery Committee. There was always a rolled-up map that stood in the corner of his home office. When unrolled, this map showed all the plots of the graves in the Jewish cemetery. Each year, he would ask for someone else to take on this volunteer position, but he was always told, "Alex, there is no one else who can go into a grieving home, like you can, and with compassion and understanding, help a family pick out a site for their family member who had just passed away, and help them figure out a payment plan." So my dad would sigh and take it on for another year.

With these memories in my psyche, and with the sadness of Abraham in my heart in this parasha, my husband and I purchased two burial plots in the Garden of David, at Eastlawn, Bet Shalom's cemetery, just about a year ago. Like Abraham, we bought plots of Jewish sanctified ground.

He and I now have peace of mind (which Abraham had to achieve at a very mournful time), knowing that none of our children—or either of us—would not have to do this sad chore, along with so many other duties that befall people when there is a death in the family. So instead of feeling morose about this task, my heart began to actually feel lighter. David and I chose our own resting places for eternity.

It is not easy to address our own mortality, but, at age sixty-seven, the two of us must acknowledge that we have currently lived more years than we have yet to live in the future. Since we have resided in Tucson for eleven years at this point, and our children are scattered all over the US, there is no more-perfect place for us to lay our mortal remains than here with the wonderful friends we have made at Bet Shalom and in Tucson.

So I'll end this D'var Torah by asking you to consider these *mitzvot*:

1. Give yourselves peace of mind.
2. Let your family be relieved of their task (as Abraham was not).

3. Choose your plot of sanctified ground, rather than have someone do it for you.
4. Help Bet Shalom fiscally.

Perhaps I should have worn sneakers and a cardigan, because I am going to a finish by saying, "Won't you be my neighbor … for eternity?"

Now I wonder where Mr. Rogers is resting, and did he purchase his plot before his demise?

Shabbat Shalom!

A Third D'var Torah for Chayyei Sarah

Today's Torah portion is entitled Chayyei Sarah, meaning the "Life of Sarah." Some of you may remember that I have spoken about this parasha twice before. In one talk, I urged you to purchase burial plots while you are still alive. This will make it easier on your family, as they will not have to do this when grieving, as we read that Abraham had to do to secure a burial place for his beloved Sarah.

The first time I delivered a D'var Torah for Chayyei Sarah, I spoke about how wise Abraham was to pay for the Cave of Machpelah as a purchase from the Hittites, even though Ephron wanted to gift him the burial spot. I likened this to the early chalutzim of the last century who bought parcels of land of what is now Israel. Much of the money for these purchases came from the blue boxes of the Jewish National Fund that every Jewish home used as a pushke. Indeed, these *deeds,* gave them lawful *deeds* to the land!

So what should I speak about this morning? When rereading these verses, I seemed to be stuck on the title: Chayyei Sarah, the Life (or Lifetime) of Sarah. When I think of what I know from reading about her in the Torah, it is not always what one would expect of a matriarch. She laughs when she hears she will have a child in her old age, and then she denies that she laughed when questioned by the Lord. Maybe that's why she is reminded of her slight deceit by having to name that child "Laughter," or Isaac.

Then, because of her extreme jealousy, she imperils Hagar and Ishmael by banishing them into the wilderness. If not for the intervention of G-d, Sarah might have become a murderess.

But, in her favor, we know she can make wonderful cakes for strangers when demanded, at merely a moment's notice. And from the grief that Abraham shows upon her demise, we know she was indeed beloved, so she must have had many endearing qualities that we can just surmise. Why would generations of female infants be named Sarah if she weren't a revered role model?

So I would like to think that Chayyei Sarah reminds us to celebrate life, even as we mourn the loss of that person. Actually, in many religions, memorial services are now called celebrations of life.

My mother passed away more than thirty years ago, and I can still remember being at her funeral with my brother and my sister. We were sitting in a small anteroom in the funeral parlor in Saratoga Springs, New York. We started talking about Mom, who died way too early, in her midsixties. Naturally, we spoke of her huge good heart and how beloved she was in our community, both Jewish and secular. She was a reference librarian and the director of the public library. I guess I was the only teenager I knew who could not complain about my mother to my friends, because they all loved her: she helped them with all their school reports!

My mother absolutely could not swear. When riled or annoyed, the worst she could come out with was "Fiddlesticks!" When we three children spoke of this, we burst out laughing, sitting there in that little anteroom off the main funeral assembly room.

Well, the funeral parlor director burst through the door, a look of horror on his face. "You should not be laughing! What will the people out here think? They are gathered for a funeral, a solemn occasion!"

33

Chastised, we meekly quieted down.

In retrospect, I think what we did was proper and befitting my mother's life. We were celebrating her life! Laughter is, in so many ways, akin to crying. Indeed, sometimes we laugh until we shed tears. Both laughing and crying are good therapy. The body relaxes, and pent-up emotions are released.

Each of us has good qualities, as well as some we would rather forget. Each of us has quirks and foibles, and if these are remembered with fondness and humor, then our lives are celebrated.

Perhaps Sarah will be forever linked to laughter, or Isaac. She tried to hide her immediate reaction of laughter to the news she would have a child. She was human like the rest of us. She wasn't perfect, and maybe this is a lesson: even a matriarch can stumble once in a while.

So when we celebrate the life of Sarah, let's do so with a smile, or even a chuckle, as we acknowledge that a sense of humor is what makes each of us so human. And if you have a bad day, or someone takes that parking space you were zooming in on, well, just say, "Fiddlesticks!" Look for the next space, and remember to smile … or even laugh!

Shabbat Shalom!

D'var Torah for Va Yishlach

Just this past week, I was privileged to hear Avraham Infeld speak at a luncheon. He talked about Judaism as a family, not just as a religion. As a family, we are comfortable with each other, we are protective of each other, and we care for each other.

This is true, but in some families, brothers do not speak to each other. Jealousies cause fences to be erected. But, hopefully, over the course of a lifetime, breaches are repaired, and the connections are made anew.

In Va Yishlach, we see this from the very beginning of the parasha. Jacob has left the house of his father-in-law, who wasn't totally honest with him for a number of years, and in his journey away from Laban, he encounters his twin brother, Esau, whom he, Jacob, had wronged in the past. Nervous about this meeting, Jacob divides his household into two camps, each to go in a separate direction, so that if there were to be warfare, at least half his household might survive.

This reminds me of my in-laws. They used to live half the year in Switzerland and half the year in New Jersey because of to my father-in-law's job with Longines Wittnauer Watch Company. In the late 1940s and early '50s, when the children were small and not in school, my father-in-law would fly to Europe with his son on one plane, and his wife would fly with their daughter on a separate flight. This way, if one plane went down, half the family would survive.

When it comes to family preservation, some things never change.

Happily, the encounter between Jacob and Esau is a peaceful one, even joyful, and the rift between the twin brothers is healed.

Also in this parasha, we read of the momentous struggle of Jacob and a divine being. Jacob's name is changed to Israel, meaning "one who struggles with G-d." So we might consider that the people of Israel are a family that struggles with each other from time to time.

The parasha goes on to tell us of the defilement of Jacob's daughter Dinah, about which Anita Diamant wrote the book *The Red Tent*. Once again, the theme of family plays a part in this story, as Dinah's brothers, Simeon and Levi, wreak vengeance on all the men in the family of Hamor and Shechem. I am actually rather horrified at the mass murder that occurs here. A little overkill, don't you think?

Actually, I am glad there are only three patriarchs in the Jewish religion. Because of their jealousy, these same two sons of Jacob, with many more of their brothers, will later sell their younger brother, Joseph, into slavery. Not a noble deed to be done within a family, for sure. Besides, it would substantially increase the length of the Amidah if we had to add twelve more names to the prayer!

All of this leads me to another thought about family. On Shabbat, we put our hands on the heads of our sons to bless them for Menashe and Ephraim. These are the sons of Joseph, who was innocent of the Dinah episode, and, obviously, of his own sale into slavery. Jacob's sons were more than a bit reprehensible. We do not want our sons to mimic their behaviors, so we look to Joseph's sons as models.

So I will leave you with this thought: which of your family members could use a visit or phone call as a nice Chanukah gift for you, and for them?

Shabbat Shalom!

D'var Torah for Vayeshev

This week's Torah parasha, Vayeshev, means "He Lived." This is actually referring to Jacob, who settled, or lived, in Canaan. But if we take it out of context, we might say the parasha is more about Joseph, Jacob's son. The fact that "He lived" is remarkable, in that there were various times in his life when he teetered on the brink of disaster.

This parasha could easily be a perfect dissertation for a sociologist or a psychologist because it deals in family dynamics, such as parental favoritism, extreme sibling rivalry, near fratricide, and lying to parents. What a perfect setup for years of counseling!

It makes you wonder why the Torah would tell this story of such a dysfunctional family. Joseph is a tattletale, encouraged and favored by his father. His brothers hate him and nearly murder him, and then lie about it to their father, causing much grief. Why are we told this story? Is it to make us feel better about the transgressions we all do in regard to our own family members? Is it to make us realize that even one of our patriarchs is only human like we are? Maybe, but I don't think so. I have another suggestion.

For more than forty-four years, I had a mother-in-law who was a difficult woman. I could not do anything to please her, and what I did do, often repelled her. For instance, I joined Hadassah when I was pregnant with my first son, about forty-two years ago. She hated the thought of me spending time working as a volunteer for a nonprofit organization. She would always refer to my Hadassah work as *schnorring*. For those of you who don't know Yiddish terms, schnorring means "begging," and not in a very nice way.

She was very unhappy with me when I traveled to Israel during the first Gulf War as a member of the National Board of Hadassah. We wore gas masks and stayed in safe rooms as Scud missiles were launched into Israel by Saddam Hussein. We felt it was our job to stand by our five thousand employees in Hadassah hospitals and schools, and not just behind them, at this time of peril. My mother-in-law called me before I left to inform me that when I died in Israel, she *would not* raise my three children for me ... As if I would need her to! They had a capable father.

Anyway, why am I telling you these mother-in-law stories? And what have they got to do with Joseph and the parasha Vayeshev? I think we all can learn from negative experiences. My mother-in-law taught me how *not* to be a mother-in-law, and I hope I learned the lesson well. I hope my two daughters-in-law, and my son-in-law, have nothing to fear from me as a mother-in-law. I hope I have never said anything to cause them pain or anxiety. This I learned from having a mother-in-law who was not always so kind to me.

Similarly, perhaps we are told these stories in the Torah so that we will learn to tone it down on any favoritism we might show to one of our children, thereby keeping the hurt and rivalry at a minimum. If Jacob had not given Joseph a coat of many colors, secretly believing that Joseph was in line for greatness, perhaps his brothers might not have nearly done away with him. As it is, they threw him into a pit and sold him into slavery. Extreme, indeed, for brothers' treatment of a sibling!

As children, we are warned about the bogeyman if we don't go to sleep. As teens, we are told of the urban myth of the hook hanging off the car door handle if we go parking with a boyfriend on a dark country road. Perhaps here, as adults, these Torah stories are warning us of transgressions that we must avoid in order to lead less conflicted lives.

So think about these stories as you read them in the Etz Hayim today, either in English or Hebrew. How can these unhappy family conflicts aid you in your own family dynamics? Maybe they will spur you on to be a better mother or father, sister or brother, or even a loving parent-in-law. I know I am trying!

Shabbat Shalom!

D'var Torah for Va-Yiggash

Sometimes I think we should honor four patriarchs, instead of just Abraham, Isaac, and Jacob. Number four would be Joseph. This is especially true when we read the parasha Va-Yiggash, as we do today.

Of course, there is something to be said about making the patriarchs human, with foibles and quirks and even somewhat reprehensible actions, so that we can easily relate to them. (You remember Jacob and the birthright, don't you?) On the other hand, it is also encouraging to encounter someone like Joseph. He was betrayed by his brothers, thrown into a pit, and then sold into slavery. Wending his way to Egypt, he becomes a dream interpreter, rising to second in command of the nation, under Pharaoh. He then proceeds to save the entire country from a seven-year famine. Sounds a little bit like an Indiana Jones movie, doesn't it? Maybe he even sported a whip and a fedora at times.

Aside from overcoming insurmountable treacheries and even jail time, he also shows incomprehensible nobleness of heart. In this parasha, he begs his long-lost brothers to not be distressed at what they did to him (specifically, selling him into slavery), because he assures them that "God has sent me ahead of you to ensure your survival on earth, and to save your lives in an extraordinary deliverance" (Genesis 45:7).

Not only has he forgiven them all for what must have been a devastating personal horror, that of near fratricide, but he also finds a way to reassure them that this was G-d's will. His forgiveness of their crime is almost unfathomable, yet it is completely sincere.

The dictionary lists these words as synonyms for forgiveness: *absolution, amnesty, pardon,* and *remission.* The antonyms are *penalty, punishment,* and *retribution.* Joseph employed all the synonyms to his brothers for their crime: total absolution, amnesty, pardon, and so on. He could easily have demanded penalties, punishments, and retribution instead. But he did not. He truly forgave them all.

The word *forgiveness* has the word *give* within it. I maintain that Joseph gave his family a gift of immeasurable wealth. He gave them the unconditional love that we all expect from our siblings, parents, and children. Do you remember the movie *Love Story,* with the phrase "Love means never having to say you are sorry"? Joseph truly embodied this statement. He wanted no one to grovel and beg for his forgiveness. Instead, he gave forgiveness to his brothers as a royal offering, and he couched it in terms of it being a predestined fate from the Lord.

Through his joy in finding his family once more, Joseph showed the true nature of forgiveness. Because, when you forgive someone, your heart is lightened, and hatred flows away. Forgiveness works both ways. The forgiver receives as much as the one forgiven.

The other lesson of this story is that of the happiness experienced when reunited with family. So many of my friends have people in their families who do not speak to each other or are estranged for one reason or another. What could be more reason for an estrangement than that of brothers turning against each other and then lying to their father about it? Yet, in this parasha, through Joseph's nobility, we are reminded of how important family and reconciliation are.

If Joseph can forgive his brothers for nearly murdering him, and for making him a slave, isn't there someone in our past that we each could forgive for a much-lesser crime? And which of us has a family member who could use a phone call or a Facebook hello?

Should we start a petition to make Joseph a patriarch too? Maybe on Facebook?

Shabbat Shalom!

D'var Torah for Va-Yehi

When Lynn Saul asked me to do the D'var Torah for Va-Yehi, I pulled out my Tanakh and found the parasha. When I read about Jacob calling all his sons together to tell them what their lots in life will be, I was somewhat appalled to hear him speak so harshly to Reuben, calling him "unstable as water." Then, of Simeon and Levi's demeanors, he said, "Cursed be their anger so fierce, and their wrath so relentless."

How could a father, on his deathbed and in front of their brothers, be so uncomplimentary to his sons? And yet, as I pondered this, I also realized, *Who knows each child better than a parent?*

Those of us who are blessed with children, and have the privilege of watching them grow into adults, know precisely which child could have a quick temper (my eldest son); which is the pragmatist (my only daughter: I can always hear her say to me when I am dwelling on an error or an unkind word that might have been directed my way, "Let it go, Mom! Get over it!"); which is the sensitive one who is slow to anger and makes friends so easily (my second son.) Parents do know their children and should be able to predict their leadership abilities to some degree.

So Jacob taps Judah as a ruler, Zebulun as a seashore inhabitant (perhaps he loved sailing on the Nile!), and Dan as a governor of his people. No

43

brother escapes his father's decree. Some are praised; others are "outed" in regard to their true personalities and foibles.

These thoughts then led me to ponder the old enigma of "nature versus nurture." How could twelve brothers, all raised in the same household (or "tenthold") turn out so differently? Did they all not have the same genes? Actually, not really, since there were four mothers between them all! Did Jacob see cunning and deception as part of the makeup of some of his sons? Did Jacob remember how he had tricked his own father, Isaac, to receive the firstborn blessing instead of Esau? Perhaps, in this case, the genes of trickery had passed from him to some of his sons, and he recognized these as such.

In my own family, my three children are very different, yet very fond of and loving to each other. My oldest son has four children of his own: triplet girls, age seven, and a six-year-old son. The triplets are fraternal, and as different in size, personality, and talents as could possibly be. One is a chatterbox and flirt. Another is shy and likes to play practical jokes on people. The third is mischievous. Their brother follows his sisters' lead and will often take the rap for the misdoings of any of them. Four children in one household, all almost the same age, yet different as day and night.

When you delve into the essays and arguments and twin studies about nature versus nurture, the only apparent conclusion is that *both* play roles in the development of a child's personality and propensities. The genes can surely affect one's makeup (studies of identical twins bear this out), but how a child is raised, and by whom, and who his or her friends are, also play major roles in the definition of a child's psyche. The answer is not black or white.

Perhaps this is why Jacob called his sons together: so that all of them should hear what he believed was best for each grown child. Forewarned is forearmed. Better to know the bad with the good, in order to lead a nation. It makes me wonder, From which of these sons was the tribe that my ancestors originated? I kind of hope it was one of the kinder and more sensitive ones.

Shabbat Shalom!

Book of Exodus

D'var Torah for Shemot

The parasha this morning is the first one of the book of Exodus, where we learn about Moses and the trials of the Hebrews while they were slaves in Egypt.

In Exodus, chapter 1, verses 15 through 21, we hear about the two Hebrew midwives, Shifrah and Puah, who were instructed by Pharaoh to kill every male child that they delivered of a Hebrew woman. Pharaoh was fearful of the growth of the Hebrews in his land and felt this was a way to contain them.

The midwives "feared God" and refused to do as Pharaoh asked, saying that the Hebrew women were too vigorous and delivered their children before the midwives could arrive to help out. It makes you wonder about the intelligence of Pharaoh that he would believe such a blatant lie. But, then again, any leader who would murder his or her own people does not seem too bright. Think of Hitler and Syria's Assad! Does ultimate power lead to ultimate stupidity?

Reading about the midwives made me think of my experience with my daughter-in-law, Mitten Lowe. She chose to use a midwife to deliver her baby. Helena, was born at the Northwest Hospital Birth Center, here in

Tucson. From the moment we arrived at the center, with my daughter-in-law in labor, the midwife was there. She stayed with my daughter-in-law throughout the entire labor, all the delivery, and for many hours afterward. The midwife was calm, very competent, and soothing in her manner. It makes me remember the delivery of my own daughter. My obstetrician came running down the hospital hallway just as one of the nurses prepared to deliver my child because the doctor was almost too late. I wish I'd had the soft presence of a midwife!

The term *midwife* is derived from the <u>Middle English</u> *midwyf* (literally, "with-woman"), meaning "the woman with (the mother at birth), the woman assisting" (in <u>Middle English</u> and <u>Old English</u>, *mid* means "with"; *wif* means "woman"). In this context, the word *wife* means "woman," not "married woman." (From Wikipedia)

Midwifery training in modern times in America can consist of a direct-entry degree program, or a nurse conversion course. Midwifery training consists of classroom-based learning, provided by select universities, in conjunction with hospital and community-based training placements. Almost all states in the United States allow midwives to practice. (From MIdwives Alliance North America)

In Israel, too, midwives are commonly used for maternal care, from predelivery to postpartum care. I'd like to share with you a story that happened in Israel:

Hadassah Nurses Deliver Baby on Icy Roadside

December 19, 2013

Barbara Sofer, Israel Director of Public Relations

Hadassah, the Women's Zionist Organization of America

The century's largest winter storm in Israel is over, but it left an aftermath of icy roads. You can imagine what fearsome traffic jams materialized.

So it was on the morning of Dec. 16 on Road 443, which leads from Modiin to Northern Jerusalem, including our Mount Scopus hospital. The road was jammed. Traffic wasn't moving. Dafna Cohen, Hadassah Mount Scopus head nurse in pediatrics, was stuck at one of the crossroads. She heard a police siren and saw cars pulled over on the side of the road. Cohen could see someone was in trouble. She, too, pulled over, "I'm a nurse from Hadassah Hospital" she said. "Can I help?"

The back seats of one of the cars had been lowered. The driver introduced himself as a medic. Inside, Batsheva Shoshan was in labor. Her amniotic fluid had already broken. Her husband Ha'ari Shoshan had been trying to drive her to the hospital, but they realized they wouldn't make it. This was their 14th delivery and they knew the baby was coming fast. The medic had a birthing kit and some other medical equipment. Cohen began helping, but then she had another idea. Hadassah midwife Hanna Kasten, also from Modiin might be on her way to work, too. Where was she? Cohen called Kasten and learned that she, too, was stuck in traffic, one light behind them.

In the meantime, the baby was crowning. Cohen and the medic delivered a healthy baby girl. Suddenly Kasten came running down the road. She took over and nurse Cohen went on to the hospital. A midwife with 20 years experience, Kasten cut the umbilical cord and delivered the placenta. She gave Shoshan an IV. Outside the temperature was 35 degrees. Kasten made sure the baby was warm and that the mother was okay. An hour and a half later, an ambulance finally made it through the ice and traffic to carry Shoshan and the baby to Hadassah Mount Scopus.

In the meantime, the police had taken advantage of Kasten's presence. An additional pregnant woman was stuck on the road. Kasten ascertained that the woman was okay, and she could continue to the hospital. At last, Kasten drove to Mount Scopus, to her day's responsibilities as deputy head of nursing for the delivery department at Mount Scopus. Her first order of business was making sure that Shoshan and Baby Girl Shoshan were safe and sound.

Nice story, isn't it? Some people might say that the oldest profession in the world is that of ladies of the night, but I think that the profession of midwife, which has endured from biblical times to the present, may just beat that one out. Perhaps, at least, they are tied for that claim!

Shabbat Shalom!

D'var Torah for Bo

Today we read the parasha Bo. *Bo* is the command form of the verb meaning "to go" or "to come." My broad interpretation of it might suggest that Moses was hoping that Pharaoh would "come around" so that the Hebrews could "go."

This portion of the Torah focuses on the last three severe plagues that befall the Egyptians because G-d has hardened the heart of Pharaoh. It makes you wonder, If Pharaoh's heart had not been hardened, would he have let the Hebrews leave Egypt sooner? There has been so much written about this over the centuries that I doubt I could say anything too different, but I will just give you one thought of mine to see if you think it makes sense.

When a person has a heart attack, some of the heart muscle becomes damaged and may die. Eventually, scar tissue forms over it. Perhaps we could think of it as a hardened area, for it no longer works as a heart muscle should; it no longer beats properly to send the blood throughout the body. So when G-d hardened Pharaoh's heart those many times that Moses and Aaron came to ask for freedom for their people, perhaps Pharaoh's heart became damaged little by little, as if from a heart attack. Surely, after the last plague when he lost his firstborn son, he must have felt as if his heart had been ripped apart.

So even though we read of Pharaoh's heart being hardened, thereby making him more stubborn and relentless, maybe it was also being set upon by minor heart attacks.

In the January 2013 issue of *Science Daily,* David H. Adams wrote, "Survivors of heart attacks are three times more likely to develop depression during the first six months after their heart attack, than people with no heart disease."

Maybe Pharaoh was also developing depression as a result of these heart hardenings. Surely, Pharaoh was plunged into a darkness of soul after the last of the ten plagues.

So forgive me if I use this as a segue into another part of this parasha, particularly that of the plague of darkness. Our Etz Hayim on the bottom of pages 376 and 377, goes into great detail about the plague of darkness, where the land is enveloped in darkness for three days. People could not see one another. It says that perhaps this was not a physical darkness, but, rather, a spiritual or psychological darkness, a deep depression. The word *melancholy* comes from a Greek root meaning "dark mood." When people are in deep depression, they have no energy to move or care for anything or anyone—not even themselves.

So we may have Pharaoh in a depression from his hardened heart, which may be like the effects of having a heart attack; and we have the Egyptian people in a possible depression-induced darkness. A very sad state, indeed, especially to then be hit with the loss of their firstborn.

It is no wonder they finally let our people go!

But in case you are all feeling a bit down from this D'var Torah discussion, I will leave you with a tidbit to buoy you up. On the same page (377) of the Etz Hayim I found an intriguing item in regard to depression and its opposite: the lifting of darkness.

It states, "In Jewish legal discussion defining how early one may recite the morning prayers, 'dawn' is defined as 'when one can recognize the face of a friend.' When one can see other people and recognize them as friends, the darkness has begun to lift."

I find this to be lovely. It connects an unpleasant physical occurrence with a comforting one. You need a friend to have a true dawning of light, whether from the sun or from the heart. And even a person who is blind can feel the face of a friend and have a dawning of the soul.

Hopefully, none of us will have hardened hearts or damaged hearts. May this year of 2014 be filled with beautiful Arizona dawns, good friends, and good health.

Shabbat Shalom!

D'var Torah for Terumah

The theme of my D'var Torah today is *acceptance and belief.*

Terumah means "gift" or "offering." The Israelites were told by Moses to offer up precious metals, yarns, fine linen, goat hair, tanned ram skins, dolphin skins (where did *they* come from, in the desert?), acacia wood, oil, and lapis lazuli and other precious stones. All of these items were to be used to make a sanctuary, an ark for the Lord. I have often wondered why they had such precious objects with them when they left so quickly from Egypt that they did not have time to even let their bread rise. Nevertheless, they were burdened with all of these rich materials. It does give us pause! But, as I said before, we are asked to *believe and accept,* so it must have been so. Actually, I have learned that the riches they carried with them were given to them by the Egyptians so that the Hebrews would leave before more plagues occurred.

No less than three times in Terumah we read that fine twisted linen strips of cloth are to be embroidered with blue, crimson, and purple woolen yarns, or to have blue yarn loops attached to the linen pieces. As soon as I read this, I thought of two other passages, in Leviticus 19:19 and Deuteronomy 22:11, where we read of the prohibition of wearing wool and linen together, called *shatnes.* So my brain leaps to answer this mystery: a mere mortal should not wear on his body that which Moses (through the Lord) commands should be made for the Tabernacle.

This seems like a possible answer for the question of why we may not wear a garment made of linen and wool woven together. But when I have voiced this to fellow Jews or teachers, they say, "No, we should not try to understand some of the 613 mitzvot. We must just obey them without explanations." We must *accept and believe.*

As sentient human beings, we constantly search for answers. We just want to know why, to know how come, to find reasons. We are unfulfilled when we cannot make sense of something.

In the month that has followed the horrible shootings here in Tucson, we have searched blindly for some reason for the deaths and the wounds, both physical and mental, for someone or something to give us the definitive answer. Was Jared Loughner so mentally unbalanced that he was completely without morals, without decency, without a shred of feeling for his fellow human beings? Was it the ease with which he was able to purchase a Glock and thirty-one bullet clips that made the crime so simple to commit? Were our state's gun laws to blame? Were the hate groups he espoused on the internet to blame? What is the final reason for this unspeakable act of violence?

Maybe the answer is that there is no single answer. Maybe in this case we must also *accept* that there is no answer—no matter how much we pull away from that concept. Maybe we just have to *believe* that goodness will prevail, in spite of acts of horror.

So if we *accept and believe,* as we do with shatnes, and we do not wear linen and wool together, then what do we do to *accept and believe* when a nine-year-old girl is murdered or a respected judge is killed or a beloved congresswoman is gravely injured?

I guess the only answer is to continue to do mitzvot, to try to make our world, during the short time each of us is in it, a little bit better for those around us and for those who follow us. We have to *accept and believe* that each mitzvah we do may somehow compensate for acts of evil and insanity.

Shabbat Shalom!

D'var Torah for Ki Tissa

This week's Torah portion, Ki Tissa, literally means "When you take." It is the longest parasha in the Torah, and it starts out innocently enough, referring to the taking of the sum of the children of Israel in the desert, to total all who have come out of Egypt. In the book of Numbers, there is also a census taken, but in that instance it is for military strength, and only the able-bodied men of a certain age are counted. In Ki Tissa, everyone from the age of twenty is counted. I am going to be optimistic and assume the women were counted here as well. (Hah!) Each person, rich or poor, was to contribute one-half of a shekel toward the furnishings of the Tent of Meeting. I can't help but wonder, if all the people of Israel were slaves in Egypt, why were some wealthier than others?

Anyway, as I read this parasha, I really get into it because it speaks of my artist hero, Bezalel, and how he was given divine talents to use to make everything Moses said the Lord required for the ark and its adornments. So even though I am in awe of Bezalel's enormous craftsmanship, I read with humbleness that everything he was able to create was because of the gifts of ability that the Lord had given him. Indeed, what he made for the worship of the Lord is only born through the gift of the Lord to his brain, his hands, and his imagination. It was all given by G-d.

It gives me pause because, as you all know, I enjoy art and craft work myself, mainly because I take joy in the creation of a good piece of art, whether it be a paper craft, a jewelry piece, a drawing, a needlework, or a calligraphic picture. When something turns out well, I am uplifted: my serotonin is flowing, my blood pressure is lowered, and I am satisfied. What I must remember is that the piece of art I have created is all G-d's. It is from divine talents that each of us is able to create, to work, to perform. My joy in forming a piece of art must be equal to the realization that the talents I have received from my Creator gave me the prowess to do so. Henceforth, I will try to temper any pride with thankful humbleness.

From this calm beginning of the parasha, we segue into the story of the golden calf, of Moses's and G-d's anger with the people in the desert, and of the near disaster to them all, had not Moses intervened on their behalf. If G-d had not been persuaded to accept these stiff-necked people, and to replace the tablets that Moses had smashed in anger and dismay, we would not be here in shul today. So, again, we must accept this gift from G-d of the Tablets of the Law. Just as we are given talents by G-d, so have we been given laws by G-d: to obey the Sabbath, to keep it holy, to honor our parents, and so forth.

It does our souls good to reflect on the treasures we have that G-d has shone upon us. Whether a lovely singing voice, the gift of being able to make music from an instrument, the ability to perform a life-saving operation, the gift of being a fine teacher, or a slew of other talents, our talents are not ours alone. They are gifts to us from the Lord. Just as the gift of the Tablets of the Law, and the Torah, have kept us as a people, so have our personal talents kept us as individuals. Hopefully, as we use these abilities, we not only please ourselves and our fellow human beings, we also please G-d.

Maybe just as G-d sees us using our talents to their utmost, he will think, as he does in the opening of Genesis, "And God saw that this was good."

We have G-d to thank for it all, and Moses to thank for intervening on our behalf. May you all go from strength to strength, but let's all remember from where our strengths originate.

Shabbat Shalom!

D'var Torah for Va-yak-hel-P'kudei

In this parasha (Exodus 39:22–40:38), Moses instructs the Israelites to build the Mishkan (the Tabernacle of the Tent of Meeting, to hold the Ark of the Covenant). The instructions are very specific, even down to the colors of the twisted yarns that are to be used on the hems of the robes. The artisans are not allowed the freedom to choose their own designs. Indeed, they are told to make pomegranates of twisted blue, purple, and crimson yarns on the hems of the robe of the ephod. Every detail of the ark—every metal, every tunic, every item—is commanded to be made exactly in accordance with the descriptions Moses received from G-d.

As an artist, I wonder if I might have chafed at these demands of Moses. What a control freak! But as we read paragraph after paragraph and architectural description after description, as well as embroidered cloth after embroidered cloth, we hear the same phrase no less than eighteen times: "as the Lord had commanded Moses." By the way, did anyone here pick up on the number eighteen? That could make another D'var Torah in itself!

So, I suppose, if I were an artist wandering in the desert with Moses, eating manna each day, seeing a dark cloud with lightning issuing forth every now and then sitting over Mount Sinai, and Moses asked me to get out my embroidery hoop and needles, I think I wouldn't have hesitated too long. And if he had added to each of his requests of me, "as the Lord commanded Moses," I believe I would have taken a quick breath and asked, with a mere second's pause, where I could set up the vats to dye the yarns purple, blue, and crimson. I doubt I would have needed to hear the command seventeen more times before I set to work in earnest.

Was it overkill to emphasize the command? Remember how recalcitrant these Israelites had been in the immediate past? Not too far from naughty children? Do you recall your own children as youngsters? How many times did you, as a parent, have to repeat a simple command to get something done? Yes, children need to hear requests numerous times before they sink in. Apparently, so do adults!

Even though the Israelites brought more than was necessary in precious metals, cloth, gems, and so on to make the Mishkan, they were not exactly trusted with the free will to make the ark as perfect as it must be made, without the repeated commands to Moses from the Lord for the people to follow.

So as an artist in the desert, I might have wanted a bit more leeway in my artistic designs and endeavors. But as an Israelite who had not too long ago been a slave in Egypt, I think I would have kowtowed without much protest. And what an incredible honor it would have been to be chosen to lend my skills or talents to such a noble endeavor! Of course, I doubt there were any women who actually worked on the Mishkan … but that's what daydreams are for.

Shabbat Shalom!

Another D'var Torah for Va-yak-hel-P'kudei

Today, we will be reading a double parasha: Vayakhel and Pekudei. In these two parashot, Moses assembles the people of Israel to remind them to observe the Sabbath. He then tells them in exact terms how to build the Tabernacle, or the Mishkan. The people are asked to donate all the materials for this process: gold, silver, and copper; blue-, purple-, and red-dyed wool; goat hair; spun linen; animal skins; wood; olive oil; herbs; precious stones. The Israelites are so into this project that they actually *over*give. Moses has to tell them that they have given enough.

This description of the raw materials that are needed, as well as the specifications on how to build the Mishkan, are also mentioned in the parashot Terumah, Tetzaveh, and Ki Tissa. It is almost like the age-old teachings for a speaker: tell the audience what you plan to say, then say it, and then tell them what you said. Apparently, Moses knew this admonition: people need to hear something a minimum of three times before they remember it.

What caught my attention is the appointment of Bezalel and his assistants to oversee all the artwork, crafts, and furnishings that would be needed to perfect the making of the Mishkan. Today, most artists are experts in one or two media at the most, but Bezalel must have been a pre-Renaissance man. He could work with gold, silver, wood, cloth, copper, and precious stones.

It is no wonder that there is a famous school in Jerusalem, the Bezalel Academy of Arts and Design, named for this all-around artist of biblical times. Their website states,

> Established in 1906 by artist Boris Schatz as the "Bezalel School of Arts and Crafts", Bezalel has evolved into one of the world's most prestigious art schools. The name Bezalel is synonymous with more than 100 years of Israeli art, innovation and academic excellence. Bezalel's unique strength stems from the numerous breakthroughs it has been responsible for and its ability to respond and adapt to cultural changes. It takes pride in its numerous generations of graduates – the spearhead of Israeli artists, designers and architects, in Israel and around the globe.
>
> The Bezalel Academy of Arts and Design is, first and foremost, a group of talented, inspired, and motivated artists and professionals. Both faculty and students are driven by a passion to create and by their dedication to quality and excellence. Bezalel offers an extensive and highly diversified range of creative and professional activities and curricular programs: from crafts such as ceramics and glass, jewelry making and design generally, where age-old traditional techniques are preserved alongside workshops unparalleled anywhere else in the country, through painting, sculpture and photography – which have undergone radical changes in recent decades – to the latest and most sophisticated digital tools and resources in industrial design, screen-based arts, architecture and visual communication.

Each department preserves the traditional knowledge, tools, materials and workshops collected over many decades, while using state-of-the-art software and cutting-edge technologies.

Bezalel trains and prepares its students for a life of achievement and excellence. Through interdisciplinary, inter-departmental and "basics" courses and the option of enrolling in courses in all of Bezalel's departments, our students are introduced to additional fields, outside of their specialized field, thereby enriching their artistic-design understanding.

I would say this truly follows the example of the Bezalel who was appointed by Moses to build, decorate, and perfect the Mishkan. A person must be an artist in many fields to be considered a Bezalel. In another lifetime, perhaps I will be fortunate enough to study there, in Jerusalem, in the footsteps of Moses's Bezalel.

Shabbat Shalom!

Book of Leviticus

D'var Torah for Vayikra

We leave the book of Exodus and start the book of Leviticus, with Vayikra. This parasha deals with the laws of sacrifice practiced in regard to the Sanctuary. Today, we no longer practice these laws because we no longer have the Temple.

Nevertheless, there are still nuggets of wisdom we can take away from this parasha. For instance, all persons—from the high priest and other priests, to chieftains, to the common people—are instructed on how they shall ask for forgiveness for their sins, either by sacrificing an animal of their flocks or by bringing choice meal and oil to offer up to the Lord. No one is omitted from performing expiation for their sins. But the higher in society the person is, the greater the sacrifice must be. For instance, a priest must offer up a bullock, a ruler must offer up a goat, and so on.

I also find it somewhat endearing that the person giving up the animal for sacrifice must lay a hand on the head of the animal. Commentaries say this is for two reasons: (1) to denote that it is the person's property and (2) that as the person's hands press or lean between the horns of the animal to be sacrificed, it designates that the animal is the person's substitute. But I wonder if there isn't another, much subtler reason. If I were to lay my hand on the head of a fur-covered animal, I would feel its warmth, its softness, and its vitality. I would almost be petting it. How much harder it would now be to sacrifice this living creature to expiate my own sin!

There are also phrases, such as Leviticus 5:17, that mention, "And when a person without knowing it, sins in regard to any of the Lord's commandments about things not to be done, and then realizes his guilt, he shall be subject to punishment." This reminds me of the prayers of forgiveness we ask at Yom Kippur, for those sins that we unknowingly commit against others. It seems that in both of these cases we are being covered for that which we, as humans, might do without realizing our sin. These are the actions that, indeed, make us human.

We then come to the lowest form of sacrifice: a mixture of choice flour and oil that is burned on the altar. Obviously, this is from a person who might not have any domesticated animal to be given. One commentary says that these two items represent that which has come by work: the flour comes from grown grain and must be milled, and the oil comes from olives that must be cultivated and pressed.

Every offering must be burned to offer "a sweet savour unto the Lord." I would imagine that the people themselves, not just the Lord, would also smell this offering as it wafted into the air. Just another subtle way of reminding the person of the sacrifice.

I would like to speak a little bit about the oil. Since I am not a farmer or a shepherd, if I had lived during these times in the desert, I would most likely have been one of the people offering up flour and oil as my sacrifice.

During this past Chanukah, in a Kabbalah class I am taking, Rabbi Zimmerman of the Oro Valley Chabad spent an entire hour talking about the significance of oil to the holiday. It wasn't just the miracle of the oil that lasted eight days that was important. It was important for the oil to be pure and kosher, so the oil would be holy and could be used in the Temple menorah. Oil has special properties that water does not. If you wet a cloth with water, it will eventually dry out or evaporate, and the cloth will probably be the same as before, but oil has a way of insinuating itself into every pore of the cloth, leaving a stain that is difficult to remove. Kings are not anointed with water; they are anointed with oil.

In fact, there is a direct link between oil and the soul.

Nina Amir writes this in *As the Spirit Moves Me,* a blog about Kabbalists, oil, and souls:

> Let's look at candles another way. In Judaism, we are told that the soul of a human being represents the candle of G-d. If we are using a wax candle, the wax equals the energy – the thing the flame needs to keep burning. If it were oil, the oil would equal energy. The Kabbalists would have used oil for their lamps and candles. The Kabbalists took notice when two words have the same letters or the same root. It's no wonder, therefore, that they noticed that while the Hebrew word *hashemen* means "oil," the Hebrew word *neshemah* means "soul." Notice that the two Hebrew words use the exact same letters. What does this mean to us? In the wisdom of Kabbalah, the soul equals our energy. It's our energy to do things and to get through things. It provides our potential to get through when things seem the darkest.

If the Third Temple were ever built, I can't say that I would be a proponent of animal sacrifice. But I think I *could* enjoy the fragrance of the choice flour and oil burning and making its way heavenward. How about you?

The night I came home from the class where we'd talked about the Chanukah oil, I was inspired to write a poem. I'd like to share that with you now. I have entitled it simply "Oil." It can be read in three ways. The first way is to read all the lines. The second way is to read just the lines in bold. The third way is to read all the lines except the bold ones.

Shabbat Shalom!

Oil

A drop of olive oil, glistening, gleaming,
golden seeming,
fit to anoint a biblical king;
   A viscous mass.

With a wick, a tiny flame is lit,
that liquid bit,
we scientifically admit,
   Morphs to gas.

An iridescent physicality
becomes spirituality
with a glorious vitality,
   And wafts away.

A scent lingers in the air,
unaware
that atoms once were there;
   But the soul will stay.

D'var Torah for Shemini

In this parasha, we read of the prohibition of Aaron and his sons, and all future Kohanim, from drinking wine or other intoxicants before entering the Tent of Meeting. This must surely be to prevent a tragedy similar to what befell Nadab and Abihu, Aaron's sons, for doing a sacrifice of alien fire.

About a year ago, I was asked to sit on a jury in Marana. We heard a case against a man in his midtwenties who was accused of driving under the influence of intoxicants. A neighbor observed him speeding through his residential area, and the neighbor then called the police. When the police arrived, they saw the young man's car in his father's driveway, and they called him out of his home. They proceeded to administer a field sobriety test to the young man. He subsequently failed the test.

He asked for a trial because he maintained that he had drunk a few swigs of vodka, *after* arriving home and before the police arrived: a matter of about fifteen minutes. He and his sister had been planning to go to a bar to watch a U of A basketball game. He didn't want to spend a lot of money on overpriced drinks, so he was "getting his game on" before they left. Hence, he had alcohol in his system when the police arrived.

The prosecution maintained that he couldn't have gotten intoxicated so quickly, and so he must have been driving drunk before he arrived at his father's home. Oddly enough, an expert witness *for* the prosecution, affirmed that a person can become drunk in as little as five minutes. We, the jury, discussed this statement in the jury room and decided to acquit the young man. He was declared innocent of drunk driving.

When I read of the prohibition of Aaron and his sons from drinking intoxicants before entering the Tent of Meeting, this experience I had as a juror, resonated in my mind. If a person can become drunk in as little as five minutes, that person's judgment and clearheadedness can be very quickly corrupted.

The young man who we acquitted was bear-hugged by his father when the verdict was announced. It brought tears to my eyes. Unfortunately, Aaron must have had different tears in his eyes as a result of the loss of his two precious sons. And he could not give them hugs any longer.

Shabbat Shalom!

D'var Torah for Metzora

Every few months, I send Cantor Avi a list of the Saturdays that I know I will be in town and can come to shul. He checks to see if there are any bar or bat mitzvahs or other special happenings on those dates, and then he lets me know when he'd like me to do a D'var Torah. That's why I am standing before you today.

I checked on which parasha we would be reading this morning and found Metzora.

Oy! It's that strange portion that tells of *tzara-at,* the skin eruption that is sometimes referred to as leprosy or Hansen's disease, but really isn't. It also speaks of an affliction that can occur in the walls of one's home, such as mold.

So I thought to myself, *This is going to give me tsuris.* For those of you who did not grow up with grandparents speaking Yiddish, I'll give you a little explanation of tsuris: It is variously defined as "troubles, worries, aggravation, woes, suffering, grief, or heartache." In other words, "tsuris is what nudniks have and are only too willing to share with others," according to the *Everyday Yiddish-English Dictionary.*

73

Then I looked at the Hebrew word *tzara-at* (that skin disease) and realized that if you read it with the old Ashkenazi pronunciation, it would be *tzara-as,* very close to tsuris. I'm not saying that writing this D'var Torah gave me a skin condition, but I'll admit that I did scratch my head a few times trying to figure out what to write. Luckily, this did not lead to scaly patches of skin possibly looking similar to leprosy!

In the Bible, tzara-at is actually a skin disease that can take many different forms, and particularly bad cases can manifest the disease in the clothing, belongings, and house of the afflicted, in addition to appearing on the skin. According to the rabbis, tzara-at is caused by sin. This makes it a disease like no other: part medical condition, part spiritual pathology. We read of it later, in the book of Numbers, when Miriam is afflicted with it as a result of her saying unkind words about Moses's wife, a Cushite woman.

So enough said about the tsuris I would get when writing about tzara-as. It actually came together fairly well. I read the parasha a few times and became intrigued by what the priest was to do for someone who was supposedly cured of a scaly infection, such as tzara-at. This is noted in Metzora (Leviticus 14:4): "The priest shall order two live clean birds, cedar wood, crimson stuff, and hyssop to be brought for him who is to be cleansed." The parasha goes on to tell how these items should be used and sprinkled on the person wishing to no longer be an outcast on account of the former affliction.

This same procedure is done if a house has been cleansed of the mold-like affliction. After the mold has been scraped away and has not returned, the house, too, needs sprinkling.

Today, I am going to focus my remarks on the crimson stuff and the hyssop because they intrigued me the most. One commentary said the crimson wool is like a tongue, and the evil that a tongue may speak must be halted. Also, I remember that crimson wool is one of the three colors used to adorn the high priest's garments—the other two being blue and purple. I recall my mother telling me that my paternal grandmother tied a red ribbon on my baby carriage to ward off evil spirits. My mother said it was pure superstition, but maybe it was just a carryover from the crimson stuff in the Torah.

So on to the hyssop. I did not know exactly what this was. I knew it was a plant, but I had no idea what it looked like, if it is still around today, or where it is grown. I found that it is an herb similar to mint, and it grows in Europe and the Middle East. Here is a picture of it. Then I thought it might be nice to have some here for you to touch. So I Googled "hyssop in Tucson." To my surprise, I was led to a JewishTucson.org article written by Deborah Mayaan.

I know Deborah. Do any of you know her? She is the one who reinstated for a few years the biblical water-carrying ceremony that we did each year in the Sculpture Garden at the JCC. Were any of you in those ceremonies? I was, twice.

So I read that Deborah had actually grown her own hyssop. I called her and spoke with her. Unfortunately, her plants were grown at a previous home of hers, and she did not have any fresh hyssop to give me. But she makes desert healing essences, or vibrational remedies, from the Sonoran and Middle Eastern Deserts. She suggested that I bring to you today a Jewish space-clearing formula that is in this spray bottle. It is used to clear the air, anywhere, with a scent-free mist. It is made up of biblical hyssop, palo verde leaf and twig, and citrine gemstone.

I made up the solution by adding four drops of the formula to this bottle of water. The literature that comes with the solution and spray bottle says, "A home may be misted once or twice a week to keep it clear. Misting is especially recommended after an argument or intense emotional release. A workplace may be misted daily for clear functioning."

It goes on to say that the plant ezov was used in purifying a building after discolored material had been removed (Leviticus 14:49–53). It was also used to apply blood to the doorposts at the first Passover (Exodus 12:22), in the purification of lepers (Leviticus 14:4), and in the purification ritual using the red heifer (Numbers 18:6). Deborah is fairly certain that the ezov is the same as the hyssop.

So you are welcome to see this after services and to spray it wherever you think it will do good. By the way, I tied a piece of crimson yarn around the bottle. Couldn't hurt!

Shabbat Shalom!

D'var Torah for Acharei Mot-Kedoshim

Earlier this week, Cantor Avi left me a message on my cell phone, asking me if I could prepare this morning's D'var Torah. Since I was at work, without a copy of our Etz Hayim at hand, I went to the internet to see what the parasha was. I skimmed it to see if something gave me an aha moment.

Today's portion is a double one, entitled Acharei Mot-Kedoshim. Acharei means "After Death" (referring to the death of Aaron's sons), and Kedoshim means "Holiness." It is jam-packed with any number of aha moments. I have chosen Leviticus 19:16 to talk about today.

When researching it on the internet, the source I used to read the entire parasha was Chabad.org, which translated the verse as "You shall not go around as a gossipmonger amidst your people. You shall not stand by the shedding of your fellow's blood. I am the Lord."

I cogitated about this for a few days, and I let different ideas float around in my brain in regard to these few sentences. As I've mentioned, my mother was a reference librarian, and she instilled in me the love of looking up words in the dictionary. Years ago, my husband and I gave away our encyclopedia to save space in our bookcases and in deference to the internet, where you can look things up in a trice. But I find there is something comforting about sitting at a table and leafing through a dictionary to find definitions of a word, so I still keep my heavy *Webster's* at hand.

So I looked up *gossipmonger*. It is not in *Webster's*. But *gossip* surely is. Believe it or not, it derives from "in the service of God." How strange that a gossiper would be from this source. The entry then goes on to say that a gossip is "an idle tattler of tales or groundless rumor." This resonates more with the prohibition in this verse.

Here, we are told not to tell tales of groundless rumor, and it is immediately followed by the admonition of not standing idly by the shedding of your fellow's blood. In commentaries, these two are related. If someone's reputation is harmed by gossip, it can indeed be a knife thrust into the psyche that sheds the blood of the soul. How many of you have felt the pain of words said against you, either truth or fiction? The harm is sometimes never erased.

If a person is damaged by slander, mischief, or libel, it is as if he or she has been wounded by an actual handheld weapon. That person's virtual blood is being shed.

When I came home from work, I opened my Jewish Publication Society Tanakh and found Leviticus 19:16. I then read the verse again in preparation for writing this D'var Torah. Imagine my surprise when I read this: "Do not deal basely with your countrymen. Do not profit by the blood of your fellow. I am the Lord."

Wow! A somewhat-different translation than that of Chabad.org. No wonder when two Jews get together there are often three or more answers to questions! So I went back to *Webster's*. *Basely* is defined as "meanly" or "vilely." Being mean or vile to our fellow countrymen could include speaking evilly or nastily about them.

I think both translations, in their core, express the entire idea of that is the basis of Judaism: *Do not do unto another that which is harmful to you.* This is the basis of Christianity's Golden Rule, but we had it first!

We can try to remember to think twice before bearing tales about another, no matter how juicy the gossip might be. We can try to always treat our fellow humans with kindness, so we do not wound them—either figuratively with mean words or literally with bloodshed—because these actions would be harmful to us if they were done to us. It doesn't matter which translation we use to learn from the Torah; it matters how we treat each other as human beings.

Shabbat Shalom!

D'var Torah for Kedoshim

This week's Torah portion, Kedoshim, means "Holiness." It is a listing of verses with rules for us on how to be holy, how to follow the commandments of the Lord. Some of the commandments are very familiar because they are from the Tablets of the Law that Moses brought down from Mount Sinai (such as "Honor thy Father and Mother," in verse 3, etc.). Some of them are a little more esoteric, such as the shatnes in verse 19, where we are told not to put on cloth from a mixture of two kinds of material.

There are so many different admonitions and laws in this parasha that someone like me could have a field day, going on forever discussing them. But have no fear—I am going to limit myself to just a few!

If we look at verse 16, it states, "You shall not go around as a gossipmonger amidst your people. You should not stand by the shedding of your fellow's blood." So why are these two rules so joined at the hip? It is because gossip and slander about another can act as a wound to that person. It is a knife struck into that person's good name. Indeed, in today's world of Facebook and Twitter, we sadly read of teens, and even younger children, committing suicide because of the gossip and bullying of their so-called friends. Gossip can kill. It can shed blood. I am just as eager to hear a good story as the next person, but we all, myself included, must remember that this is strictly forbidden by the Torah and that dire consequences can result.

If we also look at the second part of this admonition—"You should not stand by the shedding of your fellow's blood"—we can remember the converse of this: "To save a life is as if you have saved the world."

A few weeks ago in his D'var Torah, Cantor Avi told you about the bus trip to the Arizona/Mexico border that he, Andy Kunsberg, and I took to learn about border issues, the foremost of which is the desperate state of undocumented migrants seeking a better life in the United States. I was profoundly moved by this trip, especially seeing the water station that was set up in the middle of the harsh desert outside of Arivaca. The organization that sets up these fifty-plus stations is Humane Borders, and volunteers go every week to replenish the water tanks in a purely humanitarian effort to prevent deaths by dehydration. Since January of this year alone, more than 190 migrants have died in our unforgiving Sonora desert.

I decided I wanted to be a part of this nonpolitical effort to save lives. Verse 17 of today's parasha states, "Love thy neighbor as yourself." Verse 34 says, "The stranger who sojourns with you shall be as a native from among you, and you shall love him as yourself, for you were strangers in the land of Egypt." So with this in mind, and the Passover story fresh in my ears, I went last weekend in one of the water trucks to fill three hundred gallons of water at Byrd Camp, west of Arivaca.

I knew nothing about Byrd Camp, but the driver of the truck I was in told me all about it, and then I saw it myself. Besides Humane Borders, which provides water deliveries, there are other organizations. There are the Samaritans, who drive into the desert, looking for people who have been left behind by the groups led by illegal Coyote leaders. The Samaritans seek to find these individuals because they desperately need help: their feet are totally covered with blisters, or they have no more water and cannot continue because they are dehydrated, among other horrible circumstances. The Samaritans hope to find these people before the angel of death does.

The Samaritans transport the people they find to a medical unit in the middle of the desert, on Byrd Baylor's private property, called Byrd Camp. It is run by a third organization called No More Deaths (No Mas Muertes), and it looks like a M*A*S*H unit, with a big military-style tent with red crosses on it. Here the ailing migrants are treated to free medical care by volunteer doctors and nurses, each of whom stays a week or two at Byrd Camp. Conditions are incredibly primitive but sufficient to save lives.

Our job was to pump three hundred gallons of water from our truck into the containers at Byrd Camp because there is no water there other than what we bring. It is used for drinking, washing, cooking, medical care, and so forth. While we were there, we were asked to bring pairs of socks next time, if possible, because there is a great need for them.

Many of the migrants are not Mexicans; they are from Guatemala, El Salvador, and other Central American countries. They hop trains to take them to the border at Nogales. Then they walk for one to three days to meet with the Coyotes who take them across the border. Sadly, they are younger than you might think. Recently, a twelve-year-old girl was found in the desert with her three-year-old sister, wandering alone, left behind by the Coyote. Another young woman told of waiting in Nogales, Sonora, for another $1,000 from her family in Guatemala. She already had $6,000 to pay the Coyote, but she needed to give him another $1,000 for rape insurance!

What I heard and saw on this trip is indelibly etched into my persona, and I am eager to go on another water trip. It is a small way to help my fellow human beings, to make a tiny difference "in loving the stranger as myself." These people who are trying to cross the desert, breaking the law for what they feel is the right reason—to better themselves, to meet up with relatives here, or to provide for their families—do not get manna from heaven every day, nor do they have Moses to strike a rock to bring them water.

Instead, people like you and me must do what we can to save lives. The driver of my truck has been working as a volunteer with Humane Borders for eleven years. I did one single morning water run, and I am hooked. I am sure we can collect socks here at Bet Shalom, or checks for Humane Borders; or, if you'd like, talk to me about taking the steps to go on a water-station trip yourself.

Shabbat Shalom!

D'var Torah for Emor

Our Etz Hayim tells us that this parasha has the alternative name of Torat Kohanim (the "Priests' Manual"). Indeed, it sets the priests apart from the everyday members of the tribe. There are certain rules and obligations that the Kohanim must abide by. These are quite severe and can even have extreme punishments if not followed. This priests' manual spells them out.

For instance, even if a priest's wife should die, he cannot attend her burial. On the other hand, he may attend the burial of close family members. Why is there this discrepancy? The explanation that is given is that the priestly duties are on account of family (or birth) or, ultimately, because the priests are descendants of Aaron. Their distinctiveness is based on their forebears.

This reminds me of others throughout history who had their roles thrust on them, not by merit but by lineage. For example, the current queen of England, Elizabeth II, has held her office these many decades because she was descended from royalty. Actually, both her father, who was a stutterer (we all remember the excellent movie *The King's Speech*), and his brother, Edward VIII, who actually gave up the throne for the woman he loved, were two who never wanted the title or honor of being king. Their roles were thrust upon them by their lineage.

It makes you wonder about, and actually pity, those who have their positions determined by birth, such as the Kohanim, royalty, and even slaves. What if you were born into the family of Kohanim, but you had no desire to be a priest? How sad. And the rules were indeed stringent. They were set up as an example of the highest level of devotion to the Lord. The Etz Hayim goes on to say, "Every society needs a core of people who live by a more demanding code, to set an example for others of what is possible."

When considering this in today's society, which group comes to mind? Surely, the Catholic priests, with their rules of celibacy, prohibitions against marriage and having their own children, and so on, are examples of individuals subject a very demanding code. And yet, sadly, we know that this code is in some cases too severe, broken by many of those who vow to uphold it.

Then there are our own country's political figures who are supposed to be above board in nearly every endeavor. And, sadly, these too often have come tumbling down when caught in even a small misdemeanor. Society cannot tolerate indiscretions from those who are held as prime examples of how people should behave.

There is another group of men in the United States who take stringent vows and devote a year of their lives to service. These are the US Army guards of the Tomb of the Unknown Soldier. These men spend up to eight hours a day preparing their uniforms for their guard tours. They walk their beat, which is from a half hour to two hours (depending on the weather), even through hurricanes. They must maintain a certain waist size, and they cannot dishonor their role for their entire lives—even at the end of the one-year tour. If they violate these rules, they must give up the special badge they receive. Out of approximately five hundred men who have had this role, only nine have had to give up this badge. These soldiers choose this sacrifice in their jobs and willingly take on these duties.

But can you imagine how difficult it must have been to lead the life of a Kohane? And how lonely? To be born into this position must have been a burden of responsibility that not every male child desired. I guess I am glad that our modern Kohanim live fairly ordinary lives, although the prohibition about entering cemeteries is still upheld by many. It is no wonder that a Kohane is the first one called up to do an *aliyah*. Maybe he himself is not held up to the rigid rules of the Israelites of the desert or of Temple times, but, in this way, we still honor the memory of those early Kohanim.

Shabbat Shalom!

Midrash about Itamar

Itamar, High Priest Aaron's youngest son, rubbed the sleep from his eyes. He took his leather bucket to Miriam's Spring and filled it with cool water. Lugging it back to where the altar stood in front of the Tent of Meeting, he carefully poured the water into the copper laver, which stood on its stand between the tent and the altar. This was where his father would wash his hands before any ritual.

The morning light glistened on the surface of the water, and the copper twinkled. Itamar stared into the water, which slowly settled into a clear, quiet, mirrorlike surface. He could see his face, and above his head was the Cloud of the Lord, just above the Tent.

This was where Adonai stayed while the Israelites were in camp in the desert. He searched the reflection for any signs of fire or turmoil in the cloud. He didn't expect to see any, since it was morning, and night had ended with the dawn. Sometimes, when he awoke during the night, he could see jagged flashes of lightning as well as actual flames in the cloud. But during the daytime, it was peaceful.

Something in the water caught his eye, and he leaned in closer to see it better. His arms encircled the circular laver. His attention was riveted on the water.

"Itamar! What do you see that's so fascinating?" his father called out to him.

Itamar jumped backward, almost overturning the copper bowl.

"Father, I think I saw the presence of the Lord!" he stated with conviction.

Aaron stood with his hands on his hips, one eyebrow raised. "And what did this look like to you?"

His young son just shrugged and said, "It was so mysterious. I can't even describe it."

Aaron put his arm around his son's shoulders and gently drew him to his side. He gave him a comforting father/son hug.

Itamar turned one more time to the laver and wiggled his fingers in goodbye to the Lord.

The Cloud above the Tent of Meeting shifted a few feet to the right and then returned to its former place.

D'var Torah for Behar

There are a number of laws and decrees in today's parasha, Behar, that deal with home ownership, the seventh year resting of the land, the fifty-year jubilee, and also of how to treat your kin in a time of dire straits.

In Leviticus 25:35, we are admonished to let a kinsman who might be in financial straits, who had to mortgage his land to you, to live by your side. In other words, we do not evict our own kinsmen, and in this case, that means another Jew.

Over and over again, we are told to deal kindly with our own.

Even though slavery did exist (as it surely does today around the world), we are not allowed to enslave a kinsman. He may be in a state of indentured servitude, but it is not a forever slavery for him and his descendants.

In 25:38, following all these rules, we are reminded that the Lord brought us out of Egypt, into the land of Canaan. We were once slaves with no hope in Egypt, and this should never happen again to our people.

So let's take a closer look at slavery. It may seem as if the slave history in America is actually ancient history. After all, President Lincoln freed the slaves with the Emancipation Proclamation in 1863. There is no one alive in our country today who remembers being a slave or owning a slave. However, I would like to put forth sad examples that can dispute the fact that actual slavery does not exist.

When a worker puts in a full day's work of backbreaking labor and is paid maybe seven or eight dollars per hour, under the table, because he or she is an undocumented migrant, it is slavery. When a person does not receive a living wage and must either live on the streets or go to bed hungry at night, this is slavery. When young teenage girls and boys are kept as sex slaves or prostitutes by unscrupulous people, this is slavery. Just this June, the FBI freed 168 kids who'd been sold into sex slavery across 106 American cities. https://fox4kc.com/2014/06/23/fbi-operation-rescues-168-children-from-sex-trafficking-puts-nearly-300-pimps-behind-bars/

Since 2008, at least four thousand children have been freed from similar operations. Some of the victims are runaways; some just have awful parents. All of them are invisible, as far as mainstream society goes. And around the world it is even worse. Listen to this story out of Thailand: https://www.nytimes.com/2015/07/27/world/outlaw-ocean-thailand-fishing-sea-slaves-pets.html

> Lang Long's ordeal began in the back of a truck. After watching his younger siblings go hungry because their family's rice patch in Cambodia could not provide for everyone, he accepted a trafficker's offer to travel across the Thai border for a construction job.
>
> It was his chance to start over. But when he arrived, Mr. Long was kept for days by armed men in a room near the port at Samut Prakan, more than a dozen miles southeast of Bangkok. He was then herded with six other migrants up a gangway onto a shoddy wooden ship. It was the start of three brutal years in captivity at sea. "I cried," said Mr. Long, 30, recounting how he was resold twice between

fishing boats. After repeated escape attempts, one captain shackled him by the neck whenever other boats neared.

Mr. Long's crews trawled primarily for forage fish, which are small and cheaply priced. Much of this catch comes from the waters off Thailand, where Mr. Long was held, and is sold to the United States, typically for canned cat and dog food or feed for poultry, pigs and farm-raised fish that Americans consume.

While forced labor exists throughout the world, nowhere is the problem more pronounced than in the South China Sea, especially in the Thai fishing fleet, which faces an annual shortage of about 50,000 mariners, based on United Nations estimates. The shortfall is primarily filled by using migrants, mostly from Cambodia and Myanmar.

And here is a policy statement from Hadassah's American Affairs Department of July 2014 on Combatting Human Trafficking:

Every day, men, women and children are forced, defrauded, or coerced into labor or sexual exploitation, with 20.9 million victims of human trafficking globally. Trafficking and its related crimes not only harms the victims involved; they also undermine the social, political and economic fabric of the nations where they occur by devaluing individuals, demeaning women, and increasing violence and crime.

Sorry that this is not a pleasant topic for Shabbat. But we can be grateful that we are no longer slaves and that we know to treat each other with dignity. It is also refreshing and enlightening to realize that these have been our teachings since the time of Moses. I am proud to be part of a people who have a long history of righteousness. I definitely do not approve of slavery in any form, and I am sure you all feel the same way.

Shabbat Shalom!

Book of Numbers

D'var Torah for B'Midbar

As I've already mentioned, Lynn Saul has taught me that it is necessary to read a parasha a few times before writing a D'var Torah about it. This is in order to find some key phrase or idea, or even just a word, that touches the soul and provides a jumping-off point from which to write a personal commentary about that parasha.

So I read B'Midbar a number of times. It is basically the description of taking the census of the Israelites in the desert during the second year of their wanderings. Of course, when I read the word *census,* it pinged in my brain because we have so recently been sent census forms from our own government. And why should we be diligent in filling them out? So that we may get more congressional districts in our state, based on our expanded population. More districts mean more congressmen and women, which in turn probably means more revenue coming back to our state.

Surprisingly enough, the twelve tribes, based on the sons of Jacob, also received leadership roles, somewhat loosely based on the numbers of male members in their tribe. But what was most interesting was that each verse of this parasha contains the phrase "all who were able to bear arms." So that census was, first of all, only men, only beyond the age of twenty years, and "all who were able to bear arms."

This wasn't just a census to divide up the houses of the sons of Jacob by chieftains or leadership roles. It was a draft. These men were going to have to fight their hostile neighboring tribes throughout their wanderings, and possibly in the land of milk and honey. A good general needs to know the type of people he has under his command and how many of them there are. It turns out that there was a total of 603,550 troops. This is a pretty good-sized army. In our first Gulf War in 1991, there were 550,000 allied troops sent to free Kuwait from Iraq. So the Israelites in the desert had an army a little larger than that one, which, incidentally, also fought in the desert.

Also, when we add the digits of 603,550 together, the sum is nineteen, the number of blessings in the Amidah, our silent personal prayer to G-d. Did every one of these men of military strength combine together to make up the great power and strength of prayer when they communed with their Lord as one huge population?

You all know that I could not rest without saying, "What about the women?!" Indeed, there is no mention of women in this parasha written about the desert census. If we added the women, and young people younger than twenty years of age, no doubt, there would have been one to two million people wandering in the desert. But these individuals were not needed to make up the draft, so they were not included. Too bad they didn't know about the modern-day Israel Defense Forces, or even our US troops.

It is not surprising that this parasha falls at the very beginning of the book of Numbers. Nearly every paragraph has at least one number in it; some have more than one number.

If there was time, we could probably take each number and find a fitting Hebrew word that could equal its total. But I will leave that for those of you who love gematria (where letters and words have numeric values), which would definitely require paper and pencil, or a calculator. Definitely not a task for Shabbat!

Shabbat Shalom!

D'var Torah for Naso

When first delving into this parasha, it appeared to me to be more of the same that we expect from the book of Numbers: which families will be given certain jobs for the Israelites in the desert; who will carry the equipment for the Mishkan; which men are eligible, by name and by tribe; and so forth.

But as countless numbers of people (including me) have sat down to take pen to paper, or fingers to computer keys, they have no doubt struggled, as I have, with the discussion of the *sotah,* the woman who when accused by a jealous husband must go through a debasing ritual to prove her innocence or guilt. I immediately thought of the dunking stool for witches, another trial by ordeal:

> Between 1100 and 1700 AD the dunking stool was used to determine if someone was a witch. This method was deemed to be foolproof as it was so easy to spot the difference between a witch and a normal person:
>
> • **If the person sank or drowned, they were not a witch**. The fact that they would be dead was seen as only a minor issue compared to the benefits of being cleared of any charges of witchcraft.

- **If the person floated then they were definitely a witch** as their body must have rejected the "baptismal water". Confirmed witches would usually be burnt at the stake.

So if you were lucky, you would drown, but if you were unlucky, you would be dunked in freezing water and then burned alive!

http://craftywitchmoonstone.blogspot.com/2011/10/past-life.html

On the other hand, if someone were actually a witch, and was trained in Harry Potter's Hogwarts School, she could have eaten gillyweed to survive underwater. That woman would then be declared a nonwitch! If you do not know to what I am referring, here is the Wikipedia definition:

Gillyweed is a <u>magical</u> plant native to the Mediterranean and resembling a bundle of slimy, grey-green rat tails. When it is eaten by a <u>witch</u> or <u>wizard</u>, one grows gills and webbing between the fingers and toes. There is some debate among <u>Herbologists</u> as to the duration of the effects of Gillyweed on fresh water versus salt water, [1] but the effects of Gillyweed in fresh water seems to last about an hour.

So I guess the witch could really have the last say and fool all the people at her trial by ordeal. Sadly, I imagine, most of those dunked were not witches, and all of them perished.

In my mind, these two trials by ordeal—the one in Naso, our parasha today, which requires an accused woman to drink a concoction of dust or dirt from the floor of the Mishkan, mixed with the ink and/or paper with holy writing on it, to determine her innocence; and the witch dunking ordeal—both seem so esoteric and unscientific that I want to dismiss them as having no coherent authority to determine the guilt or innocence of a woman.

Indeed, if a woman undergoing the sotah process were to have a miscarriage, which is supposedly the outcome of a woman convicted of infidelity in Naso, I maintain it would actually be a miscarriage of justice!

So am I being irreverent to dismiss a part of this parasha when it is the written word of the Torah to which I subscribe as a Jew? If you look on page 796 of the Etz Hayim, at the bottom where Rashi comments, you will see that the Talmud tells us that "the ordeal of the sotah worked only in an age when people believed in its power to expose the guilty and exonerate the innocent. In the more cynical period of the Second Temple, it had to be discontinued."

So I guess that would make me cynical as well. Actually, there are many directions in the Torah that we no longer utilize in our modern lives. If we were to have animal sacrifices (which this parasha describes in detail as well), and a Third Temple were built in Jerusalem, PETA (People for the Ethical Treatment of Animals) would have to move its headquarters from Norfolk, Virginia, to Jerusalem, Israel! Personally, I am glad we no longer perform animal sacrifices as part of our rituals. I don't think such rituals would do anything positive for me in terms of achieving deeper spirituality.

So, yes, I'm a little bit cynical. No, I do not subscribe to every word in the Torah. But, yes, I still find the essence of my religion to be that which gives me joy, peace, and belief in the goodness of my fellow man.

And, speaking of my fellow man, what happened to the man with whom the woman accused of being a sotah was supposed to have committed adultery? Maybe he was dunked in freezing water!

Shabbat Shalom!

Another D'var Torah for Naso

So today we read the parasha Naso, which actually means "Take a Census." A fitting title for a parasha from the book of Numbers. And the beginning of this portion, indeed, talks of numbers, tribes, positions, and the like.

All too soon, though, it launches into that unfortunate ritual of the sotah, where a suspicious husband can force his wife, whom he believes has been unfaithful, to drink a bitter concoction to see if her body betrays her. We also learn, in our Etz Hayim, that this repugnant ritual was abandoned around the time of the Second Temple.

I am glad that my Jewish religion allows for corrections! I can't even imagine how laughable this ordeal would be in today's world, with all the evidence we now can produce, such as DNA and paternity testing.

So as I reject this ritual, I would like to call your attention to a ritual filled with mitzvot and much more grace. Recently, I joined a group of women from our shul who comprise the Chevra Kaddisha, the Jewish sacred burial society. I was able to help in the *tahara,* the washing of a woman's body that was being readied for burial.

This meaningful ritual, whether done by men for a deceased male, or by women for a deceased female, is filled with beautiful steps. Prayers are recited or sung as the body is washed, dressed in white linen or muslin garments that serve as a shroud, and lovingly prepared to be put in a casket. Soil from Jerusalem is sprinkled in with the body.

This ritual that has continued through the ages is one that I can accept without reservation. The actions during the tahara provide an example of a true mitzvah because the recipient cannot return the favor. Indeed, some other women will be doing this for me one day. I can publicly thank them today for this, though I can't be sure who they will be.

When my mother had a stroke back in 1981, she lingered in a hospital bed in my hometown of Saratoga Springs, New York, for nearly a week before she passed away. It was known that she would not recover. The ladies of the Chevra Kaddisha of our synagogue, Shaarei Tefillah, decided that my mother should not be alone that entire week, as she was failing. They set up a schedule of people who sat at her bedside, when my brother, sister, or I were not there. On the night that she died, we got a call at two in the morning, from Miriam Messenger, one of the ladies and a dear friend of my mother's. She told us that Mom had just passed away and that she was holding her hand at the time. Here it is, thirty-six years later, and I still recall the kindness of those Jewish women. Although it is not the job of the Chevra Kaddisha to do what they did, they performed this mitzvah for my family anyway. This just enforces my belief that when someone does a kind deed, it is remembered forever.

So here I am, paying it forward by becoming a member of our Bet Shalom Chevra Kaddisha. I knew very little about how to do a tahara, but, luckily for me, and for our shul, we have very experienced and knowledgeable people who are able to instruct newbies like me. In fact, one of the women who helped me do my first tahara has been doing tahara for more than thirty years. If any of you would like to be a member of either the men's or women's Chevra Kaddisha, which actually translates as "holy society," please speak to me or to Rabbi Avi* when he returns at the end of this month.

So I guess I was pretty tricky. Hardly even taking a new breath, I turned this talk from a despicable ritual, the sotah, to a beautiful ritual, the tahara. Please forgive me for veering from this parasha in order to make this D'var Torah one more fitting for Shabbat, where mitzvot can make your heart sing.

I know you are all waiting to see if I brought a prop with me today. Well, it would hardly be fitting to bring in a casket, so I have brought for our Kiddush today, cans of *diet* sotah! And a thank-you to Norm Rubin and Nathan Frankenberg for that pun.

Shabbat Shalom!

- When this D'var Torah was written, it was after Cantor (Hazzan) Avi had been ordained as a rabbi: thus the change in his title.

D'var Torah for Sh'lach Lecha

In today's parasha, Sh'lach Lecha, Moses chooses twelve scouts, one from each tribe, to investigate the land of Israel in order to best determine how to settle it. They spend forty days searching out the agriculture and the people of the land. Ten of them come back, praising the fruits of the soil, the humongous grapes the size of grapefruit (makes you wonder where the name grapefruit originated … maybe from this parasha?), wonderful figs, and pomegranates. Indeed, it was a land of milk and honey, which must have sounded so delightful after days of manna!

But then, they revealed a downside to their reconnoitering. The inhabitants were huge giants of men. The scouts said they felt as if they were grasshoppers compared to them. There were fortified cities, and it was a land that would devour them.

Only two of the scouts, Caleb and Joshua, gave the flip side of the coin as their story. They were overjoyed at this land of fruitfulness, and, with faith in the Lord, it could be conquered. Here is the gist of this parasha: Where is the faith that they all should have had, given their deliverance from Egypt with the mighty hand of the Lord?

G-d, in his anger at the meager faith in him displayed by the ten pessimistic scouts, declares that they will wander in the desert for forty years, until the entire generation that was freed from Egypt is gone. Only the next generations, who never knew slavery, would be able to enter the promised land.

As we remember their glass-half-empty report, can we relate it to today's Israel? If you were to visit this land of milk and honey today, would you see the residents of Sderot hiding in underground bunkers as rockets come in from Gaza? Would you see Israel still surrounded by hostile nations? Would you note the very young ages of the soldiers buried in the military cemeteries, and say, "Yes, this is a land that devours its inhabitants"?

Or would you notice the gorgeous beaches and hotels of Tel Aviv, which have become *the* place for Europeans to vacation? Would you remember that Israel is the first nation to arrive anywhere in the world where there is a natural disaster, such as with the Haiti earthquake, to provide medical care and search teams for survivors? Would you see the disproportionately high number of Israeli scientists winning Nobel prizes, or the incredible medical and technological advances that have emanated from this tiny state? Would you see the desert that has been turned into irrigated gardens of flowers and fruits?

What would you report if you were a scout for Moses today?

Rabbi Lawrence A. Englander grapples with this question:

> I believe the Torah text offers a direction toward resolving this dilemma, and it comes from the phrases that follow the two reports of the scouts. It seems that our relationship with the land is determined by what we perceive. If we focus on the good fruit that it yields, then we taste the sweet milk and honey of the Jewish State. If we become obsessed with the destructive elements in Israeli society, then our own self-image becomes diminished as well, and we see ourselves as grasshoppers.

So if we see the land as a glass half-full, if we have faith in the Lord, then the land will be sweet for us, and we will continue to be "a light unto the nations." But, more importantly, we will be a light unto ourselves.

Shabbat Shalom!

D'var Torah for Korach

I have read and reread this parasha, which deals so harshly with Korach and his followers, trying to find a phrase or paragraph or two that speak to me, seeking that aha moment.

Unfortunately, in way too many of those readings, I only could envision the horror of Korach's family and followers who were buried alive as "the earth opened its mouth and swallowed them up with their households, all Korach's people and all their possessions" (Numbers 16:32). All I could think of was *I hope that they died quickly by being immediately crushed, rather than by suffocation.* This is hardly the G-d I want to hold in my heart. Rather, I would like to revel in the G-d who is merciful and forgiving, the One who basks in delight when his people perform mitzvot. This is the G-d I searched for in this parasha. He was hard to find. He was hidden by his anger, his disappointment, his incredible power.

But I was also drawn to the image of Eleazer, the priest who took the copper fire pans, which had been used for the offerings by those who died in the fire (17:4), as they were hammered into plating for the altar. These fire pans had become evil. They had held burning incense as the last act of a rebellious band. Yet they were transformed into the plating of the holy altar, as a reminder that no one who was not the offspring of Aaron should burn incense before the Lord. Where have I heard of something being hammered like this before?

Could it be a precursor to Isaiah 2:4? "And they shall beat their swords into plowshares, and their spears into pruning hooks." Here again, implements of evil, as the fire pans had become, were beaten into useful objects that could no longer be used for wicked or harmful purposes. As the fire pans became a *sheathing* for the holy altar, so, too, would the swords and spears be *unsheathed* as weapons for the last time. From something intrinsically evil something clearly good is fashioned.

I am only human. I have not eaten of the Garden of Eden's Tree of the Knowledge of Good and Evil (עֵץ הַדַּעַת טוֹב וָרָע; : [Etz ha-da'at tov va-ra]), so I cannot truly fathom why G-d did not think that these followers of Korach could also be reshaped, molded, or psychologically beaten into useful servers of the Lord once again. Perhaps it is only a metal or steel tactile object, such as a fire pan, a sword, or a spear, that can be reshaped into something of worthiness once more. Because I am such an idealist, I would like to believe that man, too, can have "the metal" to be a good person, even after evil inclinations have emerged. Isn't that why we come to shul on Yom Kippur and beat our breasts? We, too, are trying to beat ourselves into the chosen people, into a people worthy of our Lord.

I am not so naive as to think that a few mitzvot can atone for a life that had been filled with evil, but, just as desecrated fire pans can be reshaped and transformed into something worthy of the holy altar, could not a damaged human being also be salvaged, rededicated, and transformed into a kind, considerate, helping individual who performs good deeds just for the joy of doing them? I hope you will agree with me that there is always this hope, for others and for ourselves.

So if you have done something you are not proud of and wish to perform a mitzvah to offset it, I have a suggestion for you, especially if you are a woman. For the past four or five years, there has been a group of Bet Shalom ladies, as well as a few who do not belong to our shul, who have comprised a Mitzvah Magic Circle. Kathy McGuire Rubin was the captain for these past years, but I am taking the reins for this coming year, starting this summer.

There are twenty-four Jewish families who are in need this year in Tucson. It's possible they are part of the working poor, not earning enough for a decent living wage; or, perhaps, there has been adversity or illness in the family; or one or both of the breadwinners may have lost their jobs. Whatever the reason, they need help.

Our circle will receive information about a family, up to even seven or eight members. Sometimes, it is even two or three generations of a family living together in one residence. This information is given to us by Jewish Family and Children's Services of Southern Arizona and facilitated by the Jewish Federation here. We are not told the names in the family, and they do not know who is assigned to them. There is complete confidentiality on both sides, so the family feels no embarrassment, just gratitude to the Jewish community.

Three times a year, before Rosh Hashanah, Chanukah, and Pesach, the team prepares baskets and boxes of gifts for their family. Each team member pledges to provide approximately one hundred dollars throughout the year to buy presents for the family, such as gift cards at grocery stores, clothing, school supplies for children, housewares, and the like. So it averages out to about thirty-five dollars per team member for each holiday. The baskets and gifts are decorated and wrapped in pretty paper and delivered to Jewish Family and Children's Services by a certain date. This is truly the case of one Jew helping another Jew.

As I mentioned, this year I have taken on the task of captain of the Bet Shalom Mitzvah Magic Circle. I need your help. Won't you come and tell me that you will join our team? If you aren't a woman, perhaps you will tell a wife or daughter, and ask her to help. You can also help with the advice and purchase of a gift, if you have a family member in our circle. Currently, we just have two women in our circle, and we'd love to have at least ten. Please let me know that you will join us!

So I have come a long way from Korach to Mitzvah Magic. But the key concept here is *mitzvah*. If we continue to pile up mitzvot, the possibility of another Korach-type event will surely diminish. I realize that this is a bit convoluted in presentation, but aren't we Jews really good at this type of thinking?

Shabbat Shalom!

D'var Torah for Balak

This is the parasha of Balak, a king of Moab who is frightened by the great horde of the Israelites he sees before him. He sends for Balaam to curse these people, but, instead, Balaam is forced by the Lord to praise them. Along the way, we meet a talking donkey and an angel of the Lord.

Everyone enjoys a good story. That's why we watch movies, such as *Mission Impossible*. We will suspend disbelief in order to see a tale to its satisfying finale because we *want* to believe, even for an hour or two.

With stories in the Torah, we sometimes try to find explanations of fantastic happenings. For instance, there are present-day scholars who maintain that there is a scientific explanation for each of the ten plagues. The darkness was a fierce sandstorm; the water turning to blood was red algae that manifested itself in Egypt; and so on.

Well, in the case of Balak, one could say that perhaps the donkey did not speak, but, instead, there was a very good ventriloquist nearby who threw his voice to the donkey, and it appeared to speak. And, just maybe, Balaam really wanted to curse the people Israel, but someone had hypnotized him just prior to his speeches, and he was forced to do just the opposite; and so, instead, he praised the children of Abraham. So if we search long and diligently enough, we just may be able to conjure up an explanation for any "unbelievable" story from the Torah.

But I maintain that, just as when someone gives away the ending of a good story before you finish reading it or seeing it in a movie, the charming tale is ruined. So in trying to make heads or tails of this story (particularly of a donkey's head or tail), we could lose the purity and childish delight in this parasha.

So let's suspend disbelief and go even further into believing that this could have happened, especially in a time of manna from heaven and clouds of lightning and rivers that divide and drown our enemies.

Let's be truly mystical for just a few minutes. Many of you know that the Kabbalah includes delving into gematria. I really don't know what made me do this, but I started with the word *Balak,* which is made up of a bet, lamed, and kuf. The bet has a numeric value of 2, the lamed is 30, and the kuf is 100; the total value of the word *Balak* is 132.

So I went to the internet to see whether I could find another word that has the value of 132. I found two more. One is *kabal* (kuf, bet, lamed), which actually has the same three letters as *Balak* but in a different order, so, of course, it also equals 132. The word *kabal* means "to receive."

The next word I found was *lekab* (lamed, kuf, bet). Also the same three letters in *Balak*, in another order. And 132 in total value.

Do you know what *lekab* means? *Damnation.*

So *Balak receives damnation.* All three words have the same numeric value and use the same three Hebrew letters. Each one is equal to 132. I decided not to go any further.

If we read 24:17, it says, "A sceptor comes forth from Israel; It smashes the brow of Moab." Balak, a king of Moab, receives damnation. Instead of cursing Israel, he is the receptor of a curse.

So isn't that cool? It wasn't necessary to look into this story scientifically. Instead, a little Kabbalistic approach gives just enough pause to suspend disbelief. I don't know about all of you, but I am just aching to try this again with another story that defies explanation.

Shabbat Shalom!

D'var Torah for Pinchas

Pinchas is one of the few parashot named after an individual Jew. This parasha makes a point to mention Pinchas's lineage, tracing it back to Aaron, of whom it is said, "Be of the disciples of Aaron, loving peace and pursuing peace, loving people, and bringing them closer to the Torah" (Pirkei Avot 1:12). This is very interesting in that Pinchas achieved this priestly status by killing a man, in a zealous action "for the honor of Heaven." You could hardly say that Pinchas was peace-loving in this action, but G-d considered it to be so.

Although Pinchas was the grandson of Aaron, he was not a priest. This is on account of the fact that Pinchas was born before the priestly assignment took effect. As he was not "born to a Priest," he could not be considered one. However, G-d gave Pinchas the "covenant of peace" and brought him and his descendants into the priesthood forever. Pinchas eventually became the high priest. So from his line came many more priests.

It makes you stop to consider "the power of one." We are all aware of people who have changed the course of history by just one act, as Pinchas did. If we look elsewhere in the Torah, we see Abraham turning to the belief of one deity and thereby starting the Jewish people. It took just one man to seed a nation that survives to this day, with you and me a part of it.

Consider Moses, a man with a speech impediment, who went before Pharaoh to plead for his people. He had this nice life as a shepherd in the Midian desert, and he gave it up to go back to Egypt to free the Hebrew slaves. The power of one.

Then there is the midrash about Nachshon, the man who dared to enter into the waters of the Red Sea and started the parting of those waters, when everyone else was frightened of drowning. The power of one.

And what about the power of one woman? (You knew I was going to get around to the feminist angle, right?) Take Golda Meir, Israel's first and the world's third woman to hold such an office. She was described as the "iron lady" of Israeli politics years before the epithet became associated with British prime minister Margaret Thatcher. The power of one woman.

So you knew I would speak about women as well as men, and many of you would expect me to mention Hadassah as well. I will not let you down! As a young woman, Henrietta Szold was in love with a man she worked with. Her love was not returned; he just considered her a colleague. So Henrietta took that unrequited love and turned it into the Daughters of Zion, a study group that started in 1912 and ultimately sent two nurses to Jerusalem to help the people there. In the past hundred years, the Daughters of Zion became Hadassah, which has grown from those two nurses to two Jerusalem hospitals with a thousand beds and five thousand employees. Three hundred thousand American women who support Hadassah, and now many international Hadassah groups, have grown from the power of that one woman.

Indeed, even in this parasha, we read of the courage of women when the five daughters of Zelophehad petition to Moses to be granted the portion of the land belonging to their father, who died without sons. G-d accepts their claim and incorporates it into the Torah's laws of inheritance. So because they spoke up, the lines of inheritance were altered to protect women for centuries to come. In this case, it was the power of five speaking as one.

And to bring this back to modern history, I read just recently that last week was the thirty-fifth anniversary of the Entebbe Airport raid, which was led by Yonaton Netanyahu, the brother of Benjamin Netanyahu, Israel's current prime minister. Yonaton lost his life in that raid. In fact, he was the only Israeli casualty. But, from that raid, Israel grew in stature worldwide, and the world saw that one individual *can* stand up to terrorism. The power of one.

So what will each of us do with our lives? Hopefully, we will not be impelled like Pinchas to deal a death blow to uphold "the honor of Heaven." But maybe we will perform a mitzvah someday that will pay it forward to others and even to generations to come. Isn't that a lovely thought?

Shabbat Shalom!

Another D'var Torah for Pinchas

When I read the parasha Pinchas, in preparation for giving this D'var Torah this morning, once again, I was moved by the plea of the five daughters of Zelophehad, who stood before Moses, Eleazar the priest, the chieftains, and the whole assembly at the Tent of Meeting to plead their case.

This story has always appealed to me, not just because, as a woman, I am always on the lookout for justice to be done for the female part of our people, but because I saw a courageous action performed by these five women: Mahlah, Noah, Hoglah, Milcah, and Tirzah. It must have taken guts to come before such an august body—perhaps akin to going before the US Supreme Court.

Their father had died, but he had no sons, just the five daughters. As the portions in the land of Israel were being given out to the tribes in preparation to entering the land of milk and honey, they were asking for their family's just due. It says in chapter 27, verses 5, 6, and 7: "Moses brought their case before the Lord. And the Lord responded that their plea is just: you should give them a hereditary holding among their father's kinsman; transfer their father's share to them."

Wow! What a precedent! In *Black's Law Dictionary,* the term *precedent* is defined as "An adjudged case or decision of a court, considered as furnishing an example or authority for an identical or similar case afterwards arising or a similar question of law. Courts attempt to decide cases on the basis of principles established in prior cases …"

So these five sisters established a precedent for Jewish women (and for many other civilized nations) for centuries to come. We have much for which to thank them.

I decided to do a little research into the land-inheritance rights of women in other countries. So, with the help of Google, I looked into the rights of women in other areas and religions worldwide. Here are some of the disturbing things that I learned:

In parts of the Middle East and North Africa, property and inheritance matters are largely governed by Shari'a law, which says that a woman's share is half that of a man when there are both male and female heirs. While religious law does not prevent women from owning assets, in some areas, women who are widowed or abandoned by their husbands may cede their share of family land to their brothers in exchange for economic support. Therefore, both laws and economic realities faced by women in many parts of the Muslim world reduce the likelihood that women own real property.

There is also much ignorance about the laws, with both men and women. Some women do not even know they can own land or inherit it. In Gaza, the majority of women are being denied their inheritance rights. The Women's Affairs Center found that 88 percent of those surveyed claimed to have been denied their inheritance. Two-thirds said they would not request aid to restore their legal rights. There are several reasons: fear of losing their children, lack of awareness of how to approach legal aid organizations, and family pressure to give up their rights. Many Palestinian women are paid off by other members of the family with a one-lump sum and forced to relinquish any rights they may have to an estate.

This problem exists in the West Bank as well, and it is more a matter of culture than religion. Usually, the family of a widow's late husband would prefer to see inheritance pass to the deceased brothers and sons rather than to the widow. Land is very important in the Palestinian community, and they don't want land to go to another family if the man dies.

So we can see that the precedent established by the Zelophehad daughters is far from universal. And, even to this day, in areas right next to Israel, women are denied land inheritance, if not by law, then through ignorance or fear. I think that all of us who believe in the equality of men and women should say *kol hakavod* to these brave women.

Shabbat Shalom!

D'var Torah for Masei

In today's parasha, Masei ("These Are the Journeys"), nearly all the reading is a retelling of the journeys in the desert. But toward the end of the parasha, there are specific references to the cities that the priests will govern, including the six cities of refuge. These cities were <u>Golan</u>, <u>Ramoth</u>, and <u>Bosor</u>, to the <u>east</u> of the <u>Jordan River;</u> and <u>Kedesh</u>, <u>Shechem</u>, and <u>Hebron</u> on the western side. I guess you might find it ironic that Hebron was once a city of refuge!

The idea behind the cities of refuge was to have places where people could find sanctuary or safety. In the Torah, such places were intended for individuals who committed unintentional murder. The issue here is blood vengeance. Numbers 35:16–21 explains that a person committing murder should be put to death (as murder violates the sixth commandment). Additionally, a member of the family of one who was intentionally murdered can act as the executioner. The kinsman carrying out this duty is the blood-avenger. But if the murder was an accident, the accused is allowed a trial to decide whether the murder was intentional. If the assembly finds in the person's favor, that person could reside in one of the cities of refuge until the high priest dies. At this point, the person would be free to return home (Numbers 35:28). If the person should leave the city before that time, it would open him or her up to retribution by the blood-avenger.

During the Middle Ages, the church was used as a place of asylum. This practice may have been rooted in this biblical text that we are reading today. Also, the Bible suggests that grabbing the horns of the altar gave a person safety (Exodus 21:12–14; 1 Kings 1:50–51). Because the altar was sacred, shedding blood would desecrate it; therefore, a person grasping the horns of the altar was safe. In recent times, asylum has moved away from sacred space and into the political realm. For example, just think of embassies within foreign countries, where political asylum can be found.

Today, the term *sanctuary city* has a much different meaning: it designates cities in which law enforcement is not allowed to ask about immigration status when arresting a person. These cities include Washington, DC, Los Angeles, Chicago, New York, and Detroit. There was a recent case here in Tucson as well. You probably remember this for this past May (as reported by Paul Ingram/Reuters):

> "A Mexican immigrant who took refuge in Tucson's Southside Presbyterian church to avoid deportation from a country where he has lived illegally for over a decade and raised a family, can stay in the United States," a federal official said.
>
> Daniel Neyoy Ruiz, 36, had been ordered to report for voluntary deportation in May. But in a high-profile challenge to U.S. immigration policy he instead turned to a Tucson church whose leaders were involved in a movement to give sanctuary to Central American refugees in the 1980s.
>
> After spending nearly a month in the church, Neyoy Ruiz was notified by immigration officials on Monday that he had been granted a one-year stay, which can be renewed annually and includes a work permit. A U.S. Immigration

and Customs Enforcement spokeswoman confirmed a stay of removal had been issued.

"I cried," Neyoy Ruiz said of the decision granting him a stay, which had been twice denied previously. "I cried out of happiness and we hugged each other knowing that this was done."

As I was researching modern cities of refuge, I came across the term *ICORN*. ICORN is an independent international organization of member cities and regions, offering safe havens for persecuted writers; advancing freedom of expression; defending democratic values and promoting international solidarity. ICORN stands for International Cities of Refuge Network.

The ICORN Charter states the following:

Everyone has the right to freedom of opinion and expression; this right includes freedom to hold opinions without interference and to seek, receive, and impart information and ideas through any media and regardless of frontiers. Any persecuted writer can apply to become an ICORN guest writer. The applicant is either:

a) At risk as a direct consequence of his/her writing – whether in danger of being killed, abducted, physically attacked or "disappeared".

b) Sentenced to (or at risk of being sentenced to) a prison term by the authorities in his/her country as a direct consequence of his/her writing.

c) Unable to express him/herself freely through his/her writing for fear of persecution due to actual or probable actions of the government or nongovernment entities of the country where he/she resides."

Here are the countries listed as having at least one ICORN city: the Netherlands, Spain, Norway, Belgium, Italy, Denmark, Sweden, Germany, Poland, Slovenia, Mexico, United Kingdom, France, and Iceland. I did not find the United States or Israel on the list.

So you can see how one idea of our Torah has been translated throughout the centuries to signify *refuge,* not just for unintentional murder but also for fear of harm because an individual's writings, to sanctuary in an embassy, to sanctuary in a religious institution. Those six cities of refuge from today's parasha have morphed into basic human rights. And, sometimes, refuge involves leaving the home nation to go to another country that offers safety. Just this past week, during the constant rockets falling into Israel even during cease-fire truces, we read that more than a thousand immigrants from France have made aliyah to Israel. They know they will have refuge from persecution in Eretz Yisroel, and, to them, it is safer to be there, even while under attack from Gaza, than to be in France.

It is no wonder that the word for refuge in this parasha is *miklat.* Besides meaning "refuge," the root of miklat (the letters kuf, lamed, tet) has two other meanings: "absorption" and "integration." So, besides giving a safe haven to the refugee, they place of safety must also be one where that refugee will be absorbed and integrated into society. I think there are many government officials in our own country who do not know what the words *refuge* and *refugee* actually mean.

Shabbat Shalom!

Book of Deuteronomy

D'var Torah for Va-Ethannan

This parasha (Deuteronomy 3:23–7:11) is jam-packed with admonitions and rules from Moses to the Jewish people who have been wandering in the desert for nearly forty years. They are about to cross the Jordan River and finally reach the promised land "flowing with milk and honey" (6:3). But even as Moses tells them how their lives must be conducted for generations to come, it is a bittersweet passage, for it begins with Moses pleading with the Lord, once again, to be able to go into Canaan. Such *chutzpah!* But how many of us, as children, also pleaded with our parents even after they said no to us? Even Moses was human and hoped that the Lord would relent and change his mind.

It is interesting that the passages read, "But the Lord was wrathful with me on your account and would not listen to me" (3:26). Moses puts the blame of his not going into Canaan onto the Jewish people. Is this where Jewish guilt first started? Moses is assigned to a lonely death on Mount Pisgah, while the children of Israel are able to go into the holy land. Wow! What a guilt trip! I don't think too many Jewish mothers can top that one!

Before he goes away to his demise, Moses firmly reiterates the Ten Commandments. The Sh'ma is also in this parasha. Moses tells the people G-d's words: "Hear O Israel" (6:4). G-d is speaking directly to the people, telling them to listen, to take heed, to remember his words, admonitions, and rules, and his covenant with the patriarchs. This passage is said three times daily by pious Jews the world over. We Jews are bound together from these biblical times to the present, from times of prosperity through times when the Sh'ma was on the lips of Holocaust martyrs, straight through to this very morning. There are Jews throughout the world saying these very words today and, hopefully, for generations without end. Also, hopefully, in good times rather than horrific ones.

There is another passage that resonated within me as I read it: "It is not because you are the most numerous peoples that the Lord set His heart on you and chose you-indeed you are the smallest of peoples" (7:7). I have often marveled at the tiny percentage of Jews in the world. Isn't it about 1 percent or so? Yet we thrive. Wherever you wander, you can find a fellow Jew and be at ease with one of your own. We Jews are to be found in every profession, often at the top of the heap. Have you seen the email that has been circulating listing the huge array of Jewish Nobel prize winners? Is it indeed because "God chose you to be His treasured people" (7:6)? Yes, we are extremely small in number, but we are huge in heart, in intelligence, and in humanity. *Am Yisroel Chai.*

Shabbat Shalom!

My Name Is Moses

My name is Moses,
Brother to Miriam and Aaron.
You may have heard of me;
If so, I am rewarded.

I battled with Pharaoh
to let my people go.
Stiff-necked people plagued me;
with Canaan, I was not rewarded.

I pled with my Lord:
Let me set foot
in the promised land;
This, I was not rewarded.

In anger I whacked a rock: Twice
to get water, but once would have sufficed.
For this breach of faith in my Lord,
I was punished, not rewarded.

Not so easy: leading millions through a desert.
Not so easy: begging for a reward.
Not so easy: being Moses.
If you know my name, I am rewarded.

Another D'var Torah for Va-Ethannan

As we have seen, this parasha (Deuteronomy 3:23–7:11) is jam-packed with admonitions and rules from Moses to the Jewish people who have been wandering in the desert for nearly forty years. They are about to cross the Jordan River and finally reach the promised land "flowing with milk and honey" (6:3). But, even as Moses tells them how their lives must be conducted for generations to come, it is a bittersweet passage, for it begins with Moses pleading with the Lord, once again, to be able to go into Canaan. Such chutzpah! But how many of us, as children, also pleaded with our parents even after they said no to us? Even Moses was human and hoped that the Lord would relent and change his mind.

This makes me consider the entire idea of deeds and rewards. Moses had just spent forty-odd years dealing with a stiff-necked people, petitioning the Lord whenever they strayed to have mercy and understanding for this recalcitrant group. He had devoted a huge portion of his life to be a wandering Jew in the desert. And yet, the reward that he sought—that of crossing the Jordan River to step foot in the land of Israel—was denied to him.

Let me digress a minute and talk about a different kind of reward. When my daughter, Caren, was two and a half years old and my son, Jonathan, was five, I decided it was time to potty-train Caren. All the rage that year was a new book that claimed you could teach a child to use the potty in one day. I bought the book and read it from cover to cover. I set out to make it work. I introduced Caren to her own potty seat and told her that every time she used it, she would get an M&M. Better yet, everyone else in the house would also get an M&M when she used it. So now I had Jonathan and my husband asking her whenever they saw her, "So you gotta go, Caren?"

It took a day and a half to train Caren—and one big bag of M&M's. My smart son recruited his five-year-old friends too, so the M&M's were a neighborhood reward. Poor Caren had quite an audience that day.

This is a very definite gastronomical reward. But what was Moses's reward?

There is a Talmudic saying that advises, "The reward for the deed is the doing thereof." In other words, the satisfaction of performing a good deed is the reward. Well, I think Moses must have had a huge good feeling for all the work he had done on behalf of his people. And maybe his reward, since it was not that of attaining a personal piece of land in Canaan, was actually the immortality he has achieved for all that he performed in his life. Why are we speaking of him today, thousands of years after the fact? Is it because good deeds are everlasting?

If you are good to your fellow humans, if you take care of the planet, or if you teach someone a skill to become self-sufficient, are you not planting the seeds of continuity for people and the world? Are these not rewards to savor?

When you help someone, do you not feel at peace? Your endorphins increase, the serotonin flows, and you have created a personal therapy that has no price, no touch, no shape. But it is your reward. We can only hope that Moses felt this as well.

So, to conclude, I will pull out my bag with props for today. As you can see, I have brought little packs of M&M's for you all. This is your reward for sitting through one more of my Divrei Torah. And you don't even have to go potty to get this reward!

Shabbat Shalom!

D'var Torah for Ekev

Today we read the parasha Ekev. The word *ekev* has a few corelated meanings. One is "heel," such as the heel of a foot; another is "if." Both of them actually mean "remember what follows." *If* you follow the words and rules of the Torah, and abide by its admonitions and lessons in your life, then *what follows* will be a good life, with bounty and blessings.

The meaning of *heel* reminds us, once again, that we should follow. We train a dog to heel, or to follow. With Ekev, we are warned and cajoled by Moses, with the Lord's words, to follow the Torah and receive the reward.

Sounds easy: do as you are told, and all will be well. Those of us who have raised children have no doubt said a few times to our children, "Do it because I said so!" Maybe we even mentioned a reward if a chore or task was done well. In Ekev, we are told to do as the Lord tells us—and, yes, there will be a reward. Chapter 8, verse 11 states, "Take care lest you forget the Lord your God and fail to keep His commandments, His rules, and His laws, which I enjoin upon you today."

Lynn Saul pointed out to me that this parasha is addressed to a plural "you," as if the Lord is addressing all his people, his flock, his children.

As parents or teachers, we often set boundaries, curfews, home rules, and chores for our children, knowing they need discipline in their lives. This is not just for the benefit of us, the parents, though it does assist in parenting. But, really, it is for the safety and well-being our children. Our disciplining guides them. Similarly, in this parasha, we find our Lord setting the rules for us so that we will have satisfying lives and will live in harmony with each other.

This made me think of what it would be like if we had not been given basic rules and boundaries in which to live within humanity. I recall William Golding's book, *Lord of the Flies,* where a group of schoolboys stranded on an island degenerate into savagery. They had no rules, no discipline, no parents, no one to teach or lead them. So maybe you are thinking, *Well, they were only children, not adults like the ones Moses was addressing.*

My friend Barbara Esmond reminded me of the story of the Hawaiian island of Molokai. In the nineteenth century, the Hawaiian government sent all the people who were afflicted with the horrible disease of leprosy into exile and quarantine on this island. Leprosy was contagious, and all lepers were ostracized. Some families were broken up, and lepers in the family were sent to Molokai. In other cases, a spouse who did not have the disease chose to follow the husband or wife into exile.

The island became filled with hundreds of desperately ill people, and leprosy could last for years before a person succumbed to it. When a young Catholic priest, Father Damien, volunteered to go to live on Molokai to bring solace to the afflicted people there, he found chaos, with nothing in the way of law and order. The island was in a state of near anarchy, where the wealthiest and strongest got what little shelter there was.

Father Damien, with meager resources, improved material conditions and brought law, rules, and well-being to the patients. Sadly, he eventually contracted leprosy as well and died from the disease.

So we see, in both of these examples, that without humanity's basic laws, decency, respect for one another, and fairness in society, all of which are stressed in our Torah, humans can become base, animalistic, and cruel.

This is exactly what we are warned about in Ekev. Follow the laws of the Torah, and reap blessings, not misery.

I wish you all good blessings now and in the future.

Shabbat Shalom!

D'var Torah for Re'eh

In the Torah parasha this morning, Re'eh, the Jewish people are told about a blessing and a curse. They are given laws. They are told which animals they may eat, and which they may not eat. From here, the laws of *kashrut* are established. But as I read through it, even though I found passages of harsh dealings and admonitions about obeying the laws, I still could see a thread of kindness that seemed to permeate the parasha.

In fact, my heart warmed to see that, no less than three times, there were directions to care for the stranger, the orphan, and the widow (in 14:29, 16:11, and 16:14). And these were often linked to caring for the Levites, the priests. So it was just as important to feed and care for the high priests as it was to care for the most vulnerable in the community. Indeed, a lesson in itself.

And then, in 15:7 through 15:11, it states, "If there will be among you a needy person, from one of your brothers in one of your cities, in your land the Lord, your God is giving you, you shall not harden your heart, and you shall not close your hand from your needy brother."

I recently heard Jeanette Mare speak at a luncheon. She is the woman who started the totally Tucson kindness project of Ben's Bells. When her son,

134

Ben, died before his third birthday of a seemingly harmless cold with a croupy cough, she and her husband found their lives filled with incredible pain from day to day. She says it was only through the kindness of friends, and even the kind things that strangers would do for her, that her life began again to have meaning. These acts of kindness gave her the will to continue each day.

Now she is the executive director of Ben's Bells, of which I know you are aware. I recently signed a Ben's Bells Kindness Contract to do intentional acts of kindness. Let me emphasize that these are not random acts of kindness. Rather, they are *intentional* acts of kindness, to do my part to make this city and this world a kinder, gentler place. One of the interesting parts of the contract is a pledge to be kinder to myself, not just to others. Cool, huh?

So what are some of these acts of kindness? We've all let someone go ahead of us in line at the grocery store if they only have one or two items, and we have a full cart. We've all held open a door for someone who is following us into a store. Right? Maybe we can do more of these things. Jeanette Mare said her sadness took a turn for the better when an unknown stranger to whom she had said "good morning" one day as she passed him on the sidewalk, turned around to her and presented her with a friendship bracelet as a little gift. A small act of kindness that moved the mountain of her depression.

So if we go back and look in this parasha for those directives to be kind to those in our midst who are hurting or in dire circumstances, let us remember that even a small gift of a smile can change a person's day for the better. Or how about this: When someone calls you to make a pledge or a donation to a reputable nonprofit organization, or to your synagogue, wouldn't it just knock the caller's socks off if you actually thanked him or her for calling so that you would have the opportunity to perform a mitzvah? Perhaps, by making that donation, you would ultimately be doing what this parasha is asking you to do: be kind to a widow, an orphan, or one who is needy.

If you would like to have a sticker from Ben's Bells that says "Keep Tucson Kind," I have some here. If you'd prefer to get it after Shabbat, I will put some on the front table of the shul.

Shabbat Shalom!

Another D'var Torah for Re'eh

When Cantor Avi asked me to do the D'var Torah this morning on Re'eh, something clicked in the back of my mind. I went to my computer and saw that I had given a D'var Torah on this parasha in 2013. I read it through and decided to go in the same direction I did then, but to fully discuss one aspect of it.

In Re'eh, the Jewish people are told about a blessing and a curse. To repeat what I discussed in 2013, they are given laws. They are told which animals they may eat, and which they may not eat. From here, the laws of *kashrut* are established. But as I read through it, even though I found passages of harsh dealings and admonitions about obeying the laws, I still could see a thread of kindness that seemed to permeate the parasha. I saw threads of egalitarianism as well. In fact, my heart warmed to see that, no less than three times, there were directions to care for the stranger, the orphan, and the widow (in 14:29, 16:11, and 16:14). And these were often linked to caring for the Levites, the priests. So it was just as important to feed and care for the high priests as it was to care for the most vulnerable in the community. Indeed, a lesson in itself.

And then, in 15:7 through 15:11, it states, "If there will be among you a needy person, from one of your brothers in one of your cities, in your land the Lord, your God is giving you, you shall not harden your heart, and you shall not close your hand from your needy brother."

Let's explore each of these categories of people. In the Torah, we have often read of "the stranger." In fact, it was Abraham who first welcomed strangers into his tent. We later realized that these strangers were actually messengers from the Lord. He was being tested on his hospitality, and only a few days after having been circumcised as an adult, and an elderly one at that. Well, we know that Abraham passed the test with flying colors. He is our example. We should be kind and welcoming to strangers, not just because we are possibly being tested, but because it is righteousness, a form of *tzedakah,* to make a person welcome and comfortable in our homes and in our hearts.

We shouldn't be looking for the silver lining. Perhaps that lining is in the friendships that may develop from our kindnesses to strangers.

Now we move to the orphan and the widow. I looked up the derivation of both of these words, and they come from old English. An *orphan* is a parentless, or sometimes just a fatherless child. A *widow* is a woman whose husband has passed away. Interestingly enough, a widower is not mentioned in these mitzvot. Presumably, a man who has lost his wife is able to fend for himself. This may be true in a monetary sense, but wouldn't he be in need of emotional support and comfort as well?

But back to the orphan. When I was thirty years old, my father passed away. A year and a half later, my mother died. At my mother's funeral, my mother's sister, my Aunt May, of whom I was very fond, came up to me, and said, "You are now an orphan. I will be like a mother to you." And she hugged me. I did not think of myself as an orphan. I was married, with three children, yet she saw me as one who needed comforting, even if only in a nonmaterial way. I have to admit, I was extremely touched by her words and actions. Indeed, I remember it to this day, thirty-seven years later. I don't think she was necessarily extending comfort to me because the Torah directed her to do so; rather, it was because she was a kind, loving person. And I believe that, even in this harsh parasha, we find kindness and love.

More likely, what the Torah expects of us is that we help those two groups, orphans and widows, in a more physical, material way. See that they are fed, clothed, and sheltered, and also to ensure that they feel they are part of the community. Do not ostracize them. Do not forget them. Do not add to their sorrows by making them disappear from the community. Include them in social gatherings and in your hearts.

Now we come to the Levites. I would imagine that this tribe of Aaron, with its many rules and regulations, would be held in great esteem and awe. Whereas the Israelites were to comfort the orphan and widow, the high priest, in fact, was not permitted to come in contact with the bodies of the dead, even of his closest relatives; and he was not permitted to leave his hair disheveled, to expose it, or to rend his garments—all outward signs of mourning. So why was he included three times in this parasha, in very close juxtaposition to the needy, the orphans, the widows, and the strangers?

If we go back to the idea of tzedakah, or righteousness, I think that we will find the answer. The Levites had no land of their own. They could not produce crops. They were truly beholden to the tithe, or donations from the populace to feed them and to provide for them. Providing for those in need is the right thing to do. And, sometimes, those in need are those most revered among us.

Often when I do a D'var Torah, I come with props. Today I have no props. Just my words and thoughts for you to carry with you in your hearts. Remember the stranger, the widow, the orphan, and, if you should meet a high priest, him also.

Shabbat Shalom!

D'var Torah for Ki Tetzei

Today, we are reading the parasha Ki Tetzei. These are the final laws in the last book of Moses: Deuteronomy. The preceding laws had dealt with those concerning public officials and the nation. These laws concern individuals, families, and neighbors.

When Cantor Avi asked me to do this commentary, he said he was sure I could find in this parasha a topic of interest on which to speak. Was he ever right! Within this portion of the Torah, there are incredible opportunities to voice an opinion or raise curiosity.

So I chose a topic that has always fascinated me: shatnes. This begins in Deuteronomy 22:9, with the prohibition "You shall not sow your vineyard with a second kind of seed ..." It continues with "You shall not plow with an ox and an ass together." It finishes with "You shall not wear cloth combining wool and linen."

I have spoken about this in a past D'var Torah because I find it interesting to try to reason out these laws. Let's start with the last one, the prohibition of wearing linen and wool together, which may derive from the fact that the high priests wore these two fabrics together when they officiated at events. It is very interesting that they were directed to remove their clothes and put on ordinary ones when leaving the Temple. Also, the Mishkan was draped in linen with wool scallops. So we see that an everyday person should not dress in cloth that is sacred, used only for priests or for covering the ark.

If you have read the *Year of Living Biblically,* by AJ Jacobs, you came upon a chapter where the author has a religious specialist come to his home to peer at all his suits and sweaters, with a microscope, to see if they are kosher. Shatnes inspector is an actual profession in the ultraorthodox communities, even today.

If we regard the second rule, of not plowing with an ass and an ox together, it makes perfect sense. One animal would be stronger than the other, and it would be difficult for the weaker one to keep up.

So if we look at the first admonition of these shatnes rules, we wonder about why you shall not use more than one seed to sow a vineyard. The vineyard must be pure so that the product can be sold as such.

I have a friend who told me a story. He wanted to get a gift for an orthodox friend who enjoyed good scotch whiskey. My friend went into a liquor store in an orthodox section of New York City, and he asked to buy a bottle of scotch. He asked the proprietor for a double-malt scotch. The proprietor shook his head and wagged his finger in front of my friend's face. In Yiddish, he told him it could only be single malt. When my friend looked puzzled, the store owner merely said, "Shatnes."

Apparently, single-malt scotch is made of barley aged in oaken barrels. Double-malt scotch can be aged in barrels that have also been used for sherry, and these may have barley plus wheat used in the process. Uh-oh! Two different varieties of grain, and possibly two different barrels of product. Shatnes!

So I thought some of you might enjoy a little scotch at the Kiddush today. Here, in this plain brown wrapper, I have a bottle to share with those of you so inclined. And—you guessed it—single malt!

Shabbat Shalom!

Another D'var Torah for Ki Tetzei

We are reading the parasha Ki Tetzei today. These are the final laws in the last book of Moses: Deuteronomy. Actually, 74 of the 613 mitzvot are spelled out here. But don't worry—I am not going to speak to you about all seventy-four. I think that if I talk about three of them, it will give you enough to chew on.

One of the reasons we have a D'var Torah each Shabbat is so we can try to make sense of the teachings of our Torah. An awful lot of it seems without rhyme or reason; or, it seems anachronistic, totally out of step with our twenty-first century. So if you will bear with me this morning, I'm going to discuss these three mitzvot, *and* I'm going to give each one what I will call "Anne's add-on." You'll see what I mean in a minute.

Ki tetzei actually means "When you go." So, turning to Deuteronomy 22:6, it states, "If along the road, you chance upon a bird's nest, in any tree or on the ground, with fledglings or eggs and the mother sitting over the fledglings or on the eggs, do not take the mother together with her young. Let the mother go, and take only the young, in order that you may fare well and have a long life." (By the way, "If along the road" is a lot like "When you go," don't you think?)

This passage bothers me. I am pained to think that the mother bird, who may fly away to get food for her babies, may then come back to an empty nest. And we all know how sad that empty-nest syndrome can be when our own kids fly off to college or move out! I find this difficult to understand, but here's what I would do instead, and it would not necessarily be going against the precepts of Torah. For Anne's add-on to this verse, I would suggest you leave at least one chick or egg for Mama Bird to find when she returns to the nest. You will still have sustenance for yourself, but I doubt that the mother bird can count, and she wouldn't feel so bereft. She would still have something to nurture.

Next, I chose a topic that has always fascinated me: shatnes. This is in Deuteronomy 22:11, with the prohibition "You shall not wear cloth combining wool and linen."

I have spoken about this in past Divrei Torah because I find it interesting to try to reason out these laws. As mentioned, the prohibition of wearing linen and wool together may derive from the fact the high priests wore these two fabrics together when they officiated at events. It is very interesting that they were directed to remove their clothes and put on ordinary ones when leaving the Temple. Also, the Mishkan was draped in linen with wool scallops. So we see that an everyday person should not dress in cloth that is sacred, used only for priests or for covering the ark.

Okay, I will try not to mix linen and wool. Anne's add-on? Don't wear polyester leisure suits either!

Now, let's turn to my third example, in chapter 24, verses 20 and 21: "When you beat down the fruit of your olive trees, do not go over them again; that they shall go to the stranger, the fatherless, and the widow." The same admonition is said about harvesting your grapes. Here, we are directed to give mandatory gifts to the poor, and to widows, strangers, and paternal orphans. I don't think this needs much additional explanation. It is a clear-cut case of pursuing, through gleaning, a righteousness that cannot be denied. It is inherent in so many of our teachings, and it is one of the tenets of the story of Ruth.

So what is Anne's add-on to this? This past Tuesday evening, the Bet Shalom board voted to support Making a Difference Every Day: The

Homer Davis Project, which was started by the Jewish Federation three years ago. Homer Davis Elementary School, in the Flowing Wells School District, has 91 percent of its students living in homes below the poverty level. These students are Latino, Asian, and Native American. There's not a Jewish student among them. They all get hot breakfasts and lunches at school, provided by our government. But what do they have to eat when they get home from school? Not very much.

The project began with twenty-two kindergartners. Every Friday, they are each given a grocery bag filled with nutritious foods to take home, so there will be something in the house for them to eat over the weekend. The principal tells the story that the Monday morning after the first students had been given their bag, one little kindergarten girl came up to him and begged to know if she would get a wonderful bag like that again. He told her she would get one every Friday afternoon to take home. Wide-eyed, she asked, "Is today Friday?"

We now pack sixty-two bags every week. Those original twenty-two kids have been getting bags every Friday for three years. We actually provide boxes of food for these children for long weekends and winter and spring breaks too, when the parents come to the school to take the boxes home, filled with tuna fish cans, peanut butter, oatmeal packets, and so on.

Here's where you can help, and also perform this mitzvot of a mandatory gift for the poor that we are reading about this morning. Bet Shalom has been asked to provide 1,200 packets of oatmeal for this winter break. Every synagogue in town is providing one of the items to fill the boxes. I went to Sam's Club and bought this box. It contains fifty-two oatmeal packets that can be made with water or milk in the microwave, or by adding the hot liquid in a bowl. I am kicking off this project right now.

So this is Anne's add-on to the third mitzvot this morning. Won't you join me? We only need twenty-two more boxes. And you don't have to buy the big box of fifty-two packets. We will gladly take the smaller boxes too. But, oops, one more thing: wait until *after* Shabbat to buy the oatmeal, and bring it here to Bet Shalom.

Shabbat Shalom!

A Bissel of This and a Bissel of That

Kol Nidre Message to Congregation Bet Shalom for 2016/2017

Gut Yontev, everyone! As your copresident, along with Rosa Cohen, I am here to give you a mini state-of-the-shul message. If you have heard me give a D'var Torah on Saturday mornings, you will remember that I often bring props with me to explain the message a little more, and sometimes those props are food or beverages. Well, I am afraid that won't work on Kol Nidre night!

Instead, I will use props that are attached to my body. I am talking about those extensions of my arms, called hands! During Yom Kippur, we often curl our hand into a fist and beat our chests with repentance and fervor. Tonight, I am going to open up that fist to welcome you all to our congregation. Consider me shaking your hand right now. But since I cannot go around the room to each and every one of you, please turn to the people next to you, shake their hands, and tell them your name. Maybe you'll make a new friend!

At Bet Shalom, we are proud of the warmth, hamishness, and heart that we display. Whether you are visiting us today, are a longtime member, or are considering joining our congregation, we truly welcome you. Bet Shalom was started more than thirty-four years ago and quickly became a very active synagogue of 140 families. Over the years, that number dwindled to about fifty-nine families, and we worried about our continued existence. I'm going to leave you hanging for a minute while I use my hand again as a prop.

An ancient Arabic and Hebrew amulet is the *chamsa*. It is a hand of five fingers. If the chamsa is pointed upward with the fingers at the top, it symbolizes a "stop sign" to an adversary. In other words, it says, "No evil may enter here." With the fingers pointed down, the chamsa symbolizes G-d's goodness and blessings coming into the room where it is hung.

Congregation Bet Shalom must have had a chamsa hanging somewhere about four years ago, when Hazzan Avraham Alpert and the shul found each other!

G-d's goodness and blessings have poured into this congregation from that day forward, so that now we have about 150 families calling Bet Shalom home. Avi's charm, incredible voice, and genuine warm welcoming smile have given Bet Shalom the spiritual leader it needed. We still have a great lay leadership who lead prayers, give Divrei Torah, chant Haftorahs, and read Torah. Anyone who wants to take part in the service is welcome to do so.

Our board recognized the gift we had been given, and a little over two years ago, we urged Avi to become a rabbi. Although being a rabbi had never been on his horizon, he accepted our challenge. He has been traveling to Los Angeles Sundays through Tuesdays for two years to study for his *smicha* (ordination). This year, he is writing his thesis, and on Monday, May 29, 2017, which is also Memorial Day, Cantor Avi will become Rabbi Avi!

We will *kvell* with pride, and many of us plan to go to LA to be with him for this momentous occasion. So save the date—you're invited! We will also be holding a Tucson-wide celebration on November 4, 2017, at the Tucson JCC, to honor Rabbi Avi. Oh, in case you are worried about him being snatched away by another congregation, don't worry! Our board has signed him to a long-term contract.

So what about the other way you hang the chamsa, with the fingers pointing up, meaning "No evil shall enter here?" Have you noticed all the changes to the outside of Bet Shalom? We have two beautiful courtyards, with secure walls and, soon, beautiful gates. We will be holding events in these areas during the good-weather months. Did you also know we have a lovely garden out behind the synagogue? Thank you, Social Action Committee! No evil will enter our grounds because we are blooming with goodness!

Our board of directors, a group of outstanding people, recently met for a retreat to do some goal planning. We are targeting an increased involvement of young people, as well as a solid education program for our families. We have already started this on Saturday mornings during services for children, and early in the afternoon with our Shabbat Experience program that encompasses free education opportunities for all age groups. Our outstanding facilitators for this program are Rabbi Dr. Howard Schwartz, Dr. David Graizbord, Morah Rita Zohav, Morah Emily Ellentuck, Leah Avuno, and Bar Elkaher.

We will continue facility improvements. Did you know that Sarah Frieden, our executive director, and Avi will both soon have offices in our adjacent modular building? We also have a Beit Midrash there, a place of study. Check it out when you have a chance.

So, as you can see, no evil, only goodness overflowing! Those of you who are members of Bet Shalom already know that we are a little bit *meshuggah* when it comes to membership dues. We actually have no set rates. We just ask each member to give as much as possible. Obviously, we cannot maintain this synagogue without everyone contributing a fair share. But we leave that decision to you. You might say that we *hand* over to you the responsibility for keeping Bet Shalom viable and healthy.

So, in closing, I will continue with one more hand prop, with a nod to the Kohanim and to Leonard Nimoy. May you all "live long and prosper!"

Aleph

Aleph, the leader of letters,
A Nachshon in a sea of emptiness,
The General of a phalanx of words,
The vanguard of thoughts.

Aleph, yud vav yud;
Adonai, yud hay vav hay.
Each twenty-six,
Each giving soul to life.

From letters to words,
From words to thoughts,
From thoughts to sentences,
From sentences to paragraphs.

From paragraphs to parashot,
From parashot to Torah,
From Torah to mitzvot,
From mitzvot to a meaningful life.

Atonement

Touch your face.
Feel the place
that smiles, beguiles.
In the mirror,
Watch it yield expression.
See it shield discretion.
Eyes twinkling,
Crowfeet wrinkling.

Cover your heart.
Feel the beat
of that steady pace,
that hidden place.
You cannot abide
that dark side.
You alone
must atone.

Avinu Malkeynu

Avinu Malkeynu:
Listen. Regard. Give ear.
Will You do this for me?

Avinu Malkeynu:
Guard. Keep. Protect.
Will You do this for me?

Avinu Malkeynu:
Be gracious. Forgive. Redeem.
Will You do this for me?

Avinu Malkeynu:
Cherish. Treasure. Encompass.
Will You do this for me?

Avinu Malkeynu:
Inscribe. Grant kindness. Give health.
Will You do this for me?

Avinu Malkeynu:
Torah. Shabbat. Mitzvot.
This I will do for You.

A Kristallnacht Memory

Zaydie, look at me!
Zaydie, speak to me!

A red blossom on your white shirt is growing,
Each stitch of one buttonhole is turning crimson.
One thread follows another.

I cannot look away.
I cannot go away.

Can I run my fingers through your beard
To touch the diamonds of glass there?
The glow of the fires reminds me of Shabbas.

But your shirt is too red.
But I know you have bled.

Isaac took the Torah from your arms.
It is hidden in a safe place.
Don't worry. The Etz Chayim survives.

I will love you forever, Zaydie!
I will miss you forever, Zaydie!

Florence and Alex

A few times each summer in the 1950s, usually on a Sunday, my dad would gather the three of us children together, and we'd pile into the back seat of our Hudson. My mom and dad would be in the front, on the bench seat. No seat belts in those days. We would head out toward Schuylerville, about a half hour's drive from our home in Saratoga Springs. Mom would have packed a little lunch of hard-boiled eggs, peanut butter and jelly sandwiches, bananas, and more. Each of us children would have our bathing suits rolled tightly in a towel. A super sandy beach under a bridge across the Hudson River was our destination. We would scamper out of the car, change in the very utilitarian cinder-block bathroom/changing building, and run down to the water. Mom and Dad would sit on a grassy bluff above the beach, keeping the three of us under their eagle eyes.

As we drove to the idyllic spot, Dad would reach over with his right hand and tickle Mom's ribs. She would giggle, and we children in the back would roll our eyes and smirk. Dad would call her his pet name, Flosie, and wink at her, and she would say, "Al, not in front of the children!" You see, my parents had a love affair all their married days. Somehow, we children instinctively realized this. It was after they had both passed away that Mom's diary made it even clearer.

June 30, 1936

It is a year since Al & I first kissed and began to go "steady." So much has happened in that year and our early "pal" stage has deepened into something really fine. It is good to love and be loved. And that I am!

Al not only shows it but needs must tell it to me many times an evening. It is true I long for marriage but at times I feel that not only is courtship the loveliest period in a girl's life, but that it has made me know Al so well that it will be difficult for me to quarrel with him after we are wedded. When that day will be, I am afraid it will be a long time before I can say. But until then, I hope we can continue to love and be careful not to be ashamed of our emotional & etc. outbursts for they have wedded us into a communal state …

My parents were married on November 21, 1937. I was their third and last child, born in 1948. They both died way too young, in their late sixties, but their love never faltered. It was a beautiful example to set for their children. I can still hear my dad saying "Flo … sie" in his wooing voice, and see my mother giggling back at him. Lovely memories.

155

Pomegranates

As a young child, growing up in Saratoga Springs, New York, about two hundred miles north of the big city, I couldn't wait to ride in our Hudson, on the front bench seat (no seat belts or car seats in those days, and I have a scar under my chin to prove it). This was especially true when my dad would take me to meet my grandmother's train, the Laurentian. I can still feel the scratchy woven front seat of the car as I write this over fifty years later. It was especially uncomfortable in the summer. But it was worth it, because Grandma Kay always had delicious surprises tucked into her tan striped valise, just waiting for her three grandchildren who lived up north "in the sticks" to discover them.

Undoubtedly, there would be two loaves of black bread that would immediately be smeared with cream cheese or pot cheese for a mid-afternoon treat. And sometimes, there would be a wonderful red pomegranate, fresh from the fruit markets of Kings Highway in Brooklyn. This was such as exotic delight! We loved our grandmother's visits, even without the pomegranate, but boy, did we savor that once or twice a year fruit! Even better, we children knew that come evening time, after dinner and the dishes were done, Grandma would take out a deck of cards, and we would all play "casino," a favorite card game where there were lucky tens and special deuces. We had been saving our pennies because Grandma loved to play with a little incentive! When the cards were finished, out came the pomegranate!

She would precisely peel the thin red skin with her paring knife. Carefully, she would dole out segments to each of us on our paper napkins, and we would eat each luscious seed with exquisite delight. Was it the sweet juice or just the fact that it came from Grandma Kay that made it so yummy? It is said that there are 613 seeds in each pomegranate, equaling the number of mitzvot in the Torah, but I am afraid we never stopped to count: the crunchy juicy tidbits were just too good to devour without adding them up!

In Hebrew, the word for pomegranate is rimon. The plural is rimonim, which is also the word for the silver coverings of the wooden handles of the Sefer Torah. In fact, those two silver adornments look like beautiful pomegranates. Often, as the Torah is being removed from the ark, the fine tinkling of the silver bells of the rimonim, reminds me of the ambrosial taste of a single pomegranate seed as it hits the back of my tongue. All of my senses are awakened: the beautiful sight of the dressed Torah in velvet and silver, the remembered honeyed taste of one of the seven fruits and grains mentioned in the Torah, the music I am hearing of the silver bells, the smooth touch I feel when I hold the wooden scrolls as I am called for an Aliyah, and lastly, the very faint wisp of a parchment fragrance as the Torah is unrolled.

The dictionary states that the word pomegranate originated circa 1320, from old French, an apple with many seeds. It is from pome, meaning apple, and grenate, having grains. It also refers to: "the skirt of the high priest's blue robe and ephod was adorned with the representation of pomegranates, alternating with golden bells."

Today, health food experts extol the benefits of pomegranate juice, as being a superpower in antioxidants. I'm not surprised. My Grandma Kay was a very wise woman.

Dill-Pickled Green Tomatoes

Nothing can compare to sinking your teeth in to ripe red tomato, picked right off the vine and sprinkled liberally with salt. Every summer, my dad would herd all of us into his Hudson, and we would drive to Bullard's Orchards in Schuylerville, about twelve miles from our home in Saratoga Springs, New York. The trunk of the car was packed with empty wooden-slatted and wire-handled bushel baskets, designed to give you splinters and cut into the palms of your hands when fully packed.

We (my mom and dad, my sister (Benna), my brother (Eddie), and I) actually went to pick green, unripe tomatoes so that my mother and sister could pickle them. But each of us had a salt shaker in the back pocket of our jeans, so we could revel in the smell and exquisite taste of a wonderful ripe tomato, should we come across one in our quest for the firm green ones. And, of course, we did always find one or two luscious, ripe, red tomatoes, either among the green ones, or maybe just a few rows over among perfectly developed fruit. It is a taste and aroma you cannot possibly get from a grocery-store purchase.

We spent a pleasant hour or two filling the baskets with green tomatoes, and then we headed back home, with a bushel basket on each of our laps, and the trunk filled to capacity. Those were the days before seat belts, but, I daresay that if we had been in an accident, the green tomatoes perched on our knees and laps would have prevented us from being ejected from the car, acting as vegetarian seat belts!

Arriving home, my sister would clatter down the back-porch stairs to the herb garden she grew against the south side of the house and cut armloads of dill that she had grown there. She and my mother had given up trying to buy fresh dill in the supermarket. Out of necessity, they grew their own.

Huge kettles of water and spices were soon bubbling on the stove. The green tomatoes, water, and spices filled dozens of quart and gallon glass bottles. They would then be stored in the room in the basement that scared me every time I had to go get another jar for the dinner table. There were three things that my father required on the supper table before we could sit down to dinner: a pitcher of ice water, bread, and a bowl of dill-pickled tomatoes. These were kept on rows of crudely made wooden shelves, in a room in the basement that had a dirt floor—and spiders. Even now, I tremble with my fear of that room.

But even with that fear, I loved the tangy taste of pickled green tomatoes. I still do to this day, even though they are difficult to find. Sometimes the Fifth Street Deli or Sprouts will carry them, and I'll snatch a jar up and triumphantly take it home to my refrigerator. Invariably, though, when I go back to get a second purchase, they are gone. They are fleeting at best.

Those jars of pickled tomatoes that my mother and sister made were prized purchases at PTA sales, and they made perfect gifts to bring to a *shiva* or a housewarming. People even saved the jars and returned them to us so that more could be made the next year. They seemed to last all year long, until each summer, when we would be recruited to go back to Bullard's to pick more. None of us ever forgot our salt shaker either.

Kosher Pickled Green Tomatoes in Salt Brine (from Benna Susman Harris)

Supplies
Quart size canning jars with wide mouth lids (or Stoneware pickling crocks)
Measuring Spoons
Large Pots that can hold at least 5 gallons of water
Table Knife, not serrated
Large Measuring Cup
Waxed Paper
Large trays to put under the jars during fermenting
Firm, green tomatoes
Pickling spices
Dried Hot Peppers
Kosher Salt
Fresh Dill Plants
Garlic Cloves

Process
Sterilize canning jars and lids and covers
Fill pot with water
Add 1 Cup Kosher Salt to every 5 gallons of water
Bring salt and water to a rolling boil
Stir to dissolve salt during boiling process

Let water cool to room temperature
While cooling, clean green tomatoes

and sort by size
Place tomatoes in jars, larger at the bottom, medium in middle,
small on top levels
Add one TBLS pickling spice to jar
Add 2 pieces of dill to jar making sure they are at least
3/4 of the length of the jar
Add 2 or 3 hot red peppers to each jar
Add 2 or 3 peeled garlic cloves to each jar
Using large measuring cup, fill jar with cooled water to the top
Let sit on counter or table awhile to settle the water
Add more water as needed
With the table knife, run it around the inside of each jar
(all the way to the bottom of the jar) to get rid of any air bubbles still in the jars

Leave jars unopened at least 8 hours
Run the knife around the inside of jar one more time

Cut Waxed Paper into strips wide enough to over hang the jar openings about
3 inches on all sides, folded in half so a double thickness is on each opening

Put waxed paper on top of each jar
Place the jar band on top of the waxed paper and tighten slightly

Store jars in cool, dry, dark place for at least 4 weeks in trays
Check after 2 or 3 weeks to see if fermenting has started
After that time, the fermenting should start to be visible
It will run down the jars and there should be a pickle type aroma

Take one jar and taste one of the tomatoes. If good, remove
waxed paper, insert lid into band and tighten it down, but not too hard
unless you are going to refrigerate them immediately.

If not, leave them in the tray until ready to use, Remember though, the
longer left fermenting, the more intense the pickling taste will become.

Esther

Esther was hardly a queen;
Just a concubine at best.
She chafed at having sex
with an "unbrissed" king.

But Uncle Mordy urged her
nonetheless. He knew
that beneath her veil,
A divine plan lurked.

From her lips, courage
would form words.
From her spine,
Haman would hang.

Laud this foregone beauty,
an unlikely heroine:
royalty of the Jews.
Hail, Queen Esther.

Hamentashen

When I hear the word *Purim,* do I think of Shushan? Nope. Queen Esther? *Nyet.* Mordechai? No way. My mind immediate goes to the calendar, to figure out how many days I have left to make hamentashen. Somehow or other, I have become my family's hamentashen baker. It must have started when my children were little, and we made them together. Now my children are grown, with their own broods of kids, but I am still designated as the hamentashen provider for all three of their families. Even though they all have the recipe and know how to make them!

Luckily, I learned to perfect these fruit-filled delicacies way back in the mid-1970s when I lived in Princeton, New Jersey. A wonderful Hadassah friend, Marion Roehmer, taught a bunch of us twentysomethings the rudiments of the task. Best of all, she gave us the recipe that has been my stalwart friend for these forty-plus years. It is a never-fail, always-perfect cookie dough. It even works for my granddaughter Helena Ziporah's gluten free–flour hamentashen, which she should be receiving today in the mail in Boulder, Colorado.

Throughout the year, I dutifully check Fry's, Safeway, and even Wal-Mart for cans of Solo kosher filling so that when Purim rolls around I am also ready to roll—in this case, the dough!

Each of my children has a favorite. Caren swears by apricot. Ethan likes raspberry. Jonathan and family are content with any flavor. His four children used to call the hamentashen "fruit-filled cookies" because their mother isn't Jewish and didn't know the right name, and their father, my son, was in the Air Force, and invariably away in Iraq, Afghanistan, or Utah, when they received my packages of goodies. As the years progressed, they became adept at saying the name, and "hamentashen" rolled off their tongues as fast as they went down their throats.

This year, my husband begged me to find strawberry Solo filling because I once found it many years ago. No luck finding it here in Tucson. But, happily, I turned to the internet, and found the mother ship of Solo fillings, a company called Sokol, in Countryside, Illinois. Minimum order is six cans, so I am set for a while!

Last week, I made sixteen dozen hamentashen in the kitchen of Congregation Bet Shalom. We auctioned them off at the Spring Festival on Sunday, and I am proud to say they brought in a tidy sum for the shul. I must give credit to my two helpers, Kamala Alpert and Susan Kendal. They are great dough rollers and pinchers.

So, in case, any of you reading this little composition have the urge to become hamentashen mavens, as I did more than forty years ago, I am happy to pass on Marion's recipe. But beware—attached to it may be a family commitment for years to come!

Hamentashen Recipe

4 eggs
1 cup sugar
1 cup oil (e.g., Wesson)
5 to 6 cups flour
2 1/2 teaspoons vanilla
1/4 cup water
1 teaspoon salt
2 teaspoons baking powder

Beat eggs in large mixing bowl. Add sugar, oil, water, and vanilla, one at a time, beating after each addition. Add salt and baking powder to flour (start with 5–5 1/2 cups flour). Add dry mixture (flour, salt, and baking powder) to egg mixture. Stir with wooden spoon until dough holds together. Knead with hands. Add more flour, as needed, to keep mixture in a ball.

Roll out with rolling pin on floured surface. Cut with round cookie cutter. Fold up two edges of circle, and put in 1/2 teaspoon Solo fruit filling. Fold up last edge of circle, and pinch closed.

Bake at 375 degrees for 15–20 minutes. Makes 5–7 dozen, depending on size of cookie cutter.

For filling, buy Solo cans of fruit filling: apricot, cherry, raspberry, strawberry, and so on. One can lasts an entire recipe. If you use more than one flavor, you'll have extra filling. I cover the can with aluminum foil, refrigerate, and use again a few days later.

Hannah and Shmuel

"Therefore have I dedicated him to the Lord."

I wonder how Hannah can just give away
a child for whom she so fervently did pray.
This Shmuel, who was "asked for of the Lord,"
She relinquished of her own accord.

As she weaned him, did she not silently weep?
Did her tears bathe him in his sleep?
He was hers for such a few years.
Isn't this a mother's worst fear?

Would Eli appreciate this longhaired gift of a son,
When wrenched from her breast this child had come?
And won't Hannah be bereft as before,
Childless again, lonely once more?

And Shmuel himself, so tender his years,
Did he sob for his mother when she should come near?
Yet he grew to be a prophet, a biblical sage,
Fostered by Eli at such a young age.

Jonah in the Belly of Sheol

(Based on the book of Jonah.)

I tried to make myself very small by hugging my knees close to my chest. I was surrounded by an almost tangible atmosphere of toxins. Should I hold my breath, or inhale the noxious fumes? Under my buttocks I felt such a thumping of a great heartbeat that I feared I would tumble off my tiny perch. Then, surely, I would be consumed by acids and chemicals whose names I would not even be able to pronounce. Was I to die by an unknown bodily secretion? Would this great gastric organ seize me and squeeze me until I was merely sustenance for a finned denizen of the seas?

But the minutes, perhaps hours (who knew how long I sat in that ebony dark?), crept on in that sinister cavern. Gradually, I came to understand that I might survive. But for how long must I suffer, smelling the digested sea creatures around me, fearing to reach out a hand in the inky miasma? I didn't know whether I wanted to perish and be consumed by this great beast, or, perhaps, live out days, weeks, or years in a complete blindness with no one to touch, speak to, or hold close. Which is worse: a miserable death or a horrid existence?

"Lord, deliver me of this creaking, heaving, unearthly prison. I will gladly do your bidding. Forgive me for my insolence and fear of carrying out your word. I have atoned with great humility. No task you might ask of me could ever compare with the possibility of years in the belly of sheol."

And after three days and three nights, "The Lord commanded the fish, and it spewed Jonah out upon dry land" (Book of Jonah, Chapter 3, Verse 11).

Jonah Poem

Why was there digestion hesitation on the part of the whale?
Did Jonah own a special charm of grand scale?
How did he sit in a pit of stomach acid for days?
Was divine intervention the prevention that sways?
If the Nineveh Cinema was XXX-rated,
Why was the fire of the Lord's ire abated?
Jonah saved the depraved people of that city;
Punishment averted, he blurted, "What a pity!"

Loving-Kindness

(Based on the silent Amidah [Source of Life and Master of Nature], *in* The New Mahzor, *p. 268.)*

When considering the phrase "You sustain the living with loving-kindness," I wonder if "the living" might refer to two groups of people: those who receive the act of loving-kindness, and those who perform that act.

For instance, yesterday morning, I was having a very early breakfast at an IHOP with Alayne Greenberg. Alayne's son, Isaac, is a captain in the US Army and currently stationed in Afghanistan. My son, Jonathan, a major in the US Air Force, just returned from a deployment in Iraq. We were meeting to plan the purchasing of items for thirty-six boxes we will be sending for Rosh Hashanah to US troops overseas. I was bringing to her car thirty-six honey bears that I had bought at a ninety-nine-cent store, as well as thirty-six cans of fuji apple slices. We were discussing what else we needed to put in the boxes, and also when we would meet to pack them up to send out to soldiers, marines, and airmen in Iraq and Afghanistan.

As we were enjoying our talk, Alayne noticed that a two-striper from the air force, in a khaki camouflage uniform, sat down across the aisle from us and ordered his breakfast from the waitress. Alayne suggested that we pay for this young man's breakfast when we checked out. I thought that was a wonderful idea.

When we went to the cash register and told the waitress of our request, she went and told the young airman, which wasn't what we had wanted. Nevertheless, he came right up to us with tears in his eyes to thank us for our deed of loving-kindness. In turn, we replied that it was as if we were "paying it forward" to our own sons in the service of their country.

So, on the drive home, I started pondering our act. Who received the greatest satisfaction from the small mitzvah we performed? Certainly, the airman was quite touched, and, surely, it made his day that two ladies, who were strangers, would treat him so kindly. But even more heartwarming to me was doing the act itself. I (and I'm sure Alayne as well) received the soul-enriching joy of performing an act of loving-kindness. I think of the phrase "a double-edged sword," but, instead, when you perform a mitzvah of loving-kindness, it is a double-sided flame of goodness that lights up the life of both the recipient and the doer of the act. I can't wait to find an opportunity to do such an act again. This time, I hope I can do it and disappear before the recipient knows who I am. It will feel even better then.

Pharaoh, Watch Out!

Pharaoh, take heed!
You know there is need.
Rivers and lakes will *bleed*.
Frogs will invade, indeed.
Pharaoh, take heed!

Pharaoh, listen to me!
Lice will create misery.
Cattle will feel agony.
A *blight* on the land will be.
Pharaoh, listen to me!

Pharaoh, beware!
Do you not care?
Boils will be a nightmare.
Hail will rain down everywhere.
Pharaoh, beware!

Pharaoh, open your ears!
Do not heed your seers.
For a *locust* swarm appears.
And *darkness* will add to your fears.
Pharaoh, open your ears!

Pharaoh, watch out!
Moses has real clout:
The *angel* of the Lord is about.
Can you afford to doubt?
Pharaoh, watch out!

Miriam's Music

Miriam.
Mere I am.
A young girl who set her baby brother afloat.
A woman who sees him now as the right hand of the Lord.

Miriam.
Mere I am.
Once a slave who still smells the algae and mud of the sea.
But stands here dry and liberated and alive.

Miriam.
Mere I am.
A human who tries not to shout with extreme exultation of victory.
While others drown in the sea of their affliction.

Miriam.
Mere I am.
Lightning has pierced the sole of my foot from the center of the world.
I tingle and shiver, and my arm reaches skyward, my timbrel quivering.

Miriam.
Mere I am.
From my throat, a keening for the dead Egyptians erupts.
From my soul, a dance for my people explodes.

Miriam.
Mere I am.
Just a woman who has experienced miracles,
With a tangle of notes that praise the Lord.

Miriam.
Here I am.
Molecules of sinew, blood, and flesh.
Playing the music for a million steps toward freedom.

Hear No Evil, See No Evil, Sing No Evil

I loved my third-grade teacher, Miss Hannah. She saw in me a budding artist and often asked me to decorate the bulletin boards for various holidays and special events. I also adored Miss Hennessey, who came once a week to teach the entire class handwriting. In third grade, we were learning cursive writing, and it was absolutely delicious for me! Maybe it was a foretaste of the calligrapher I would become in my thirties.

One other teacher came once a week to our class. Her name was Miss Allerdyce, and she taught music, which invariably meant singing songs. I reveled in singing. Even now, in my sixties, when I sing in the synagogue, it is a spiritual event for me. That's how I felt, even as a nine-year-old.

In December, during that third-grade year, Miss Allerdyce came to the classroom, sat down at the piano, and informed us all that we would be singing Christmas carols. I was cool with this. It happened every year, and I knew all the words. Just before she began, with her hands poised above the keyboard, she announced to me, in front of the class, "Anne Susman, you will not sing today, because you are Jewish."

175

Stunned and horrified, I sat at my desk, with my hands folded on top of it, and stared at my lap so that I wouldn't have to see the expressions of the other students around me. Of course, I could hear the charming melodies and words, but I was forbidden to open my mouth and join in. The tears rolled down my cheeks and made dark splotches on my navy-blue dress. I sat there like a stone for the entire music class. My mouth was stitched closed.

Later that evening, my mother asked me why I was so quiet and subdued. I told her what had happened in music class. Her cheeks became red, and she muttered, "Anti-Semite!" I asked her what that meant, and she said I'd learn later in life.

Indeed I did.

My Evolution of Shabbat

Shabbos. Shabbat. The Sabbath. Saturday.

To a Jewish girl growing up in Saratoga Springs, New York, in the 1950s, Shabbos was jam-packed with negatives. Can't. Shouldn't. Don't. Mustn't. Banned. Taboo. You get the picture.

Attend junior congregation services every Saturday morning. Trudge through the below-zero weather and snowdrifts, with rubber boots and freezing toes, for thirteen blocks, but don't let the rabbi see you surreptitiously take a Kleenex from your coat pocket to swipe at your running nose as you enter the synagogue, or you will be admonished for carrying something to shul on Shabbos. Better you should wipe your nose on your sleeve or mitten. Yuck!

Don't crayon, don't write, and don't watch TV. Don't drive to shul with your parents, but if you do, you'd better park across the street from the synagogue and behind St. Peter's Church so no one will see your car.

Know all the prayers, but don't expect to be asked to do an aliyah. You're a girl.

The Sabbath wasn't a day of joy. Instead, it was a day of *oy*. No wonder, when I went off to Syracuse University, I joyously decided to pledge a sorority house that had previously had no Jews.

The Sabbath day did not change much for me until I was in my thirties. In 1985, I was the volunteer arts-and-crafts director for Camp Young Judaea–Midwest, located at a rented site, Camp Nihelu, in Ortonville, Michigan. I didn't just teach arts and crafts (*melechet yad,* meaning "work of our hands"). I also painted backdrops for plays, silk-screened T-shirts for the entire camp of 150-plus campers and counselors, made Shabbat decorations, and so on. Never did I appreciate Shabbat more than when I could padlock the arts-and-crafts building at five o'clock each Friday afternoon and know it would stay locked until nine o'clock on Saturday night, after Havdalah on the beach.

Not only was Shabbat a definite day of rest for me, but, at camp, it actually became the day of special treats! Friday-night dinner was always a scrumptious chicken meal, with lots of singing. Saturday-morning *tefillot* (prayers) were followed by a yummy breakfast of coffee cake and cantaloupe. The staff-versus-campers baseball game was a joyous weekly contest, where I continually saw the evidence of our teachings. Teenage CITs would deliberately flub a catch or a pitch to a baseman so that a young camper could feel the pride of making it to first base. In the afternoon, everyone was allowed to do leisure-time activities, as long as they involved being with at least one other person. So sitting and reading poetry with friends and playing Scrabble (and using number cards from a deck of cards to score with, so no writing was involved), checkers, chess, and so on—all were activities we did on the beach or on the grass under a shady tree. Shabbat truly became the antithesis of my childhood. No became *yes*.

Now I'm in my sixth decade, and I have once more found new meaning in Shabbat. At my synagogue, Bet Shalom, the once-a-month Shabbat dinner and service gives me a lovely extended family with whom to welcome Shabbat with a story, a service, and delicious homemade delicacies. I have even started coming to the Saturday-morning services, not just once a month but even more frequently.

I have learned the joy and felt the honor of writing and delivering a D'var Torah, as I delve into the parasha of the week and find personal meaning within. Because Bet Shalom is a conservative shul, women are counted as members of the *minyan* and participate in all aspects of the service. I still get nervous when asked to do an aliyah—maybe because of the psychological ban I still feel deep in my psyche in regard to women doing such a task. Nevertheless, I am learning to participate with pride. I am included rather than excluded.

The relaxation of sitting and letting the music flow over my soul, and the joining in on melodies that I remember, deliver a new focus for Saturday morning. I can drop the petty problems and demands of my job, my volunteer activities, my family commitments, and even the never-ceasing demands of my own brain. Enforced sitting still has evolved into sweet rejuvenation. What a concept Shabbat is! So now, in Tucson, as it was in camp, instead of no, Shabbat is *yes*.